UNDERSTANDING
CLIMATE CHANGE
and its Mitigation

UNDERSTANDING CLIMATE CHANGE
and its Mitigation

RANJIT CHAVAN

PARTRIDGE

A Penguin Random House Company

To order additional copies of this book, contact
Partridge India
000 800 10062 62
orders.india@partridgcpublishing.com

www.partridgepublishing.com/india

C O N T E N T S

Sooner or later, we will have to recognize that the Earth has rights, too, to live without pollution.

Evo Morales

UNDERSTANDING CLIMATE CHANGE- AND ITS MITIGATION

by

Ranjit Chavan
PRESIDENT
All India Institute of Local Self-Government

Mumbai Head Office:
Sthanikraj Bhavan

C.D. Barfiwala Marg,
Andheri(West), Mumbai-400058.
Tel. 0091-22-
26206716,26205670,26284431
Fax No. 0091-22-26288790/26235386
Web: www.aiilsg.org
Email: dg@aiilsg.org

Extension Training Centre:
M.N. Roy Human
Development Campus,
T.P.S. Road No. 12,
Behind Teachers Colony,
Bandra (East),

Mumbai – 400051.
Tel. 0091-22-26571713/14/15
Fax – 0091-022-26572115.

PREFACE

Twenty seven years have passed since the establishment of the Intergovernmental Panel on Climate Change (IPCC), the highest scientific body under the UN system for assessing the knowledge of climate change, its science, the environmental, economic and social impacts and possible response strategies. Through its five Assessment Reports the Panel has zeroed in on the human hand in causing present global warming and consequent climate change. Its voluminous reports have led to taking several measures and understanding the threat. Twenty- one Conferences of Parties have been held under the auspices of the United Nations Framework Convention on Climate Change (UNFCCC). Kyoto Protocol, the instrument among the nations to bring down the emission levels is still in operation, and its successor Agreement which has been agreed in the form of Paris Accord, to become operative from 2020. Still the specter of 2^0C rise from the pre-industrial level is looming large- the level of rise that would be catastrophic for the earth and life on the earth according to the scientists. The consequences of climate change are becoming more pronounced by the day. The international community and national governments are seized of the threat.

There is a general perception that the seriousness of the threat and the urgency to act is not reflected down in the local administration and public actions. Its concern is not seen in day to day life, when the fact is that every action of the billions of individuals makes or mars the prospect of mitigation of and adaptation to climate change. Perhaps the mass awareness and concern of the public at large is wanting. A strong public opinion and concern on this threat is needed. Equally important is that people in their daily life and mundane affairs can do much to tackle the threat through power saving, avoiding wastage of paper, water, planting trees and a host of things. (A chapter is dedicated to this in the book).

The All India Institute of Local Self Government is *inter alia*, engaged in the study, research and publications on the issues of urbanization and environment. During its 90 years of existence it has constantly kept track of the change happening in the country, in society, in urban scenario, and has constantly updated its mandate and activities. In pursuance of its objectives, the Institute has decided to bring out literature for the understanding of this threat of climate change, and the measures for its abatement. The Institute earnestly desires to make a humble contribution in spreading the knowledge and concern for climate change that is showing dire consequences the world over. Earlier in 2013 the Institute published a book entitled 'Understanding Climate Change', which was well received. Subsequently, another exhaustive book- 'Understanding Climate Change-Its Mitigation and Adaptation to It' was brought out at international level through Partridge Publishing Co. Through the feedback it is felt that an abridged version of the earlier one with low-price would also be useful in dissemination of the concern of climate change. As such, this book is another humble effort of the Institute in this direction.

I wish to re-iterate some points from the Preface of the earlier book, namely that a vast corpus of literature on climate change is published the world over; a large number of voluminous books are brought out dwelling on some or the other aspects of the phenomenon. It was observed that most of the books are written in technical jargon. There are hardly any books that put across the whole phenomenon, events, concepts, courses of action in simple non – technical language and style. This book, like its predecessor books, is an attempt to look at the huge problem in almost all its aspects, and an effort to present it in a clear, simple and non-technical language and communicative tone. As such it is an *informative* book. Awareness, dissemination of knowledge is the essential pre-requisites of any meaningful action. What global warming is, and how it sets off a chain of reactions in the global climate system has been assessed and explained by the **IPCC**. The **WMO** is a world level body, *inter alia*, providing leadership in observing and monitoring the climate and making available huge information to the countries and IPCC. The **UNFCCC** is committed to bring the countries of the world together in charting courses action. As such the enormous reports, fact sheets, graphics and publications of these bodies are the authoritative sources of information on climate change. These bodies have graciously put their huge reports, information sheets, analyses etc. on the net, for the world to have access. As such, this book **is *substantially based* on these authentic sources of highest authority.**

Besides, a number of other scientific bodies, institutions, in the UN system and outside, are engaged in very valuable climate research and are equally gracious to put their research reports on the web for the world to read them and make use of. As such, the author has referred to a number of such websites and taken the particular nuggets of information from them. Each of the sources is duly acknowledged in the respective chapter. Wherever necessary, permission for use of the information and images is duly taken. Care is taken to ensure that references are taken as permitted, and in the manner required.

I earnestly hope this book will serve its intended purpose.

Ranjit Chavan

ABBREVIATIONS

Use of abbreviations is kept at the minimum level in the book. Whenever an abbreviation is first used, its full form is given in bracket. Yet, a list of abbreviations used in the book is given below for the convenience of the reader.

AAU	Assigned amount unit (Equal to 1 metric ton of CO_2 equivalent calculated using the Global Warming Potential.
AR4	Fourth Assessment Report of the IPCC.
AR5	Fifth Assessment of the IPCC.
AOSIS	Alliance of Small Island States.
$CaCO_3$	Calcium carbonate
CAIT	Climate Analysis Indicator Tool (of WRI).
CCS	Carbon Capture and Storage.
CDIAC	Carbon dioxide Information Analysis Centre.
CF_4	Chlorofluorocarbon.
CH_4	Methane.
CLICOM	Climate Computing Project of WMO.
CMP	Conference of Member Parties (of Kyoto Protocol), held in conjunction with COP.
CO_2	Carbon dioxide.
COP	Conference of Parties (of UNFCCC) held annually.
ENSO	El – Nino Southern Oscillation.
FAO	Food and Agriculture Organization (UN)
FAR	First Assessment Report of the IPCC
GAW	Global Atmospheric Watch.
GCOS	Global Climate Observing System.

GHG	Greenhouse gas.
GGCA	Global Gender and Climate Alliance.
GOS	Global Observing System.
Gt.	Gigatonne
GWP	Global Warming Potential.
HCFCs	Hydrochloroflourocarbons.
HFCs	Hydrofluorocarbons.
IAC	Inter Academy Council (of IPCC).
ICS	International Council for Science.
INC	International Negotiations Committee (of UN).
INCCA	Indian Network for Climate Change Assessment.
IOC	International Oceanic Commission (of UN).
IPCC	Intergovernmental Panel on Climate Change.
N_2O	Nitrous oxide.
NAPCC	National Action Plan on Climate Change
NASA	National Aeronautics and Space Administration (of the USA).
NOAA	National Oceanic and Atmospheric Administration (of the USA).
NMHSs	National Meteorological and Hydrological Services.
O_2	Oxygen
O_3	Ozone
ppb(v)	Parts per billion (by volume)
ppm(v)	Parts per million (by volume)
SAR	Second Assessment Report (of the IPCC).
SAT	Surface air temperature.
SO_2	Suphur dioxide.
SPM	Summary for policy makers (of IPCC reports).

SRES	Special Report on Emission Scenarios (of the IPCC).
TAR	Third Assessment Report (of IPCC).
TFB	Task Force Bureau (of IPCC).
TGICA	Task Group on Data and Scenario support for Impact and Climate Analysis (IPCC)
UNDP	United Nations Development Programme.
UNEP	United Nations Environment Programme.
UNFCCC	United Nations Framework Convention on Climate Change.
WCDMP	World Climate Data and Monitoring Programme (of WMO)
WCP	World Climate Programme (of WMO).
WCRP	World Climate Research Programme (of WMO).
WCSP	World Climate Research Programme (of WMO).
WDCCG	World Data Centre for Greenhouse Gases.
WEDO	Women's Environment and Development Organization.
WGI	Working Group I (of the Assessment Reports of the IPCC).
WGII	Working Group II (of the Assessment Reports of the IPCC).
WGIII	Working Group III (of the Assessment Reports of the IPCC).
WIS	World Information System (Computer Architecture).
WMO	World Meteorological Organization.
WRI	World Resources Institute (Washington based).
WWF	World Wildlife Fund.

List of Figures

(Images that illustrate the content of the related text)

17	22.2	Sources of greenhouse emissions from Indian agriculture	203

List of Photos

(Images that relate to the topic)

Sr. No.	Photo No.	Content	Page No.
1	1	Global warming (Sun on the horizon)	1
2	2	Clouds in the sky	2
3	3	Climate change	18
4	7	Nest weaver bird (A delicate of biodiversity)	71
5	22	Greenery	198

List of Boxes

Sr. No.	Box No.	Content	Page No.
1	1	Forcing, What is radiative forcing	8
2	5	Global oil output	47
3	6	Humanity the enemy	65
4	8	2^0 C Tipping point not far	93
5	19	Gender, gender equality, gender equity etc.	178
6	22	Energy not consumed is the cleanest energy. Indian Prime Minister Mr. Narendra Modi	206

NB: The number of figures, photos and boxes are according to the concerned chapter, i.e. the integer used for figure/ photo or box indicates the chapter in which the figure or photo or box is included.

About the Institute

Established in 1926 as an institute for training institute for the urban local bodies, the **All India Institute of Local Self-Government,** Mumbai has come a long way to become a national level training institute having 28 Regional Centres in India, and has many specialized institutions which are its integral part. The Institute is registered under the Societies Registration Act, 1860 and the Bombay Public Charitable Trusts Act. It is a no-profit organization. It is socially motivated. Through its activities it aims to contribute to better urban management and environment protection. Its divisions are as under:

1) Regional Centre for Urban & Environmental Studies (RCUES), established in 1968 by the Government of India, in 1968, which undertakes policy research, case studies, advisory and consultancy services, specialized trainings, customized trainings, seminars, workshops and organizes study visits for experience sharing.
2) Planning and Resources on Urban Development Affairs (PRUDA), which is involved in comprehensive urban planning and management projects with the Government of India and various State Governments and urban local bodies to make urban areas much more livable spaces.
3) National Fire Academy.

4) Nrupur Institute of Nursing Science and Research.
5) National Resource Centre on Urban Poverty.
6) International Academy of Urban Dynamics.
7) International Centre for South-South Learning.
8) Advanced Centre for Sustainable Development & Urban Poverty Alleviation.
9) Academy for Women Elected Representatives.
10) GIS Services Centre.

In order to upgrade the existing programmes and knowledge resources the Institute has linkages with many government departments, reputed universities and national level/specialized institutions, which include the following-

1) Ministry of Urban Development, Ministry of Housing and Poverty Alleviation, Government of India.
2) State Governments in India.
3) Municipal Corporations, Development Authorities, Municipal Councils.
4) University of Mumbai, Saurashtra University, Yashwantrao Chavan Maharashtra Open University, CEPT University, Indira Gandhi National Open University, S.N.D.T. University, Mumbai etc.
5) Indian Institute of Technology, Mumbai, V.J.T.I. Mumbai, Tata Institute of Social Sciences, Mumbai, National Institute of Urban Affairs, New Delhi, Yashwantrao Chavan Academy of Development Administration etc.
6) National Institute of Public Co-operation and Child Development, New Delhi.
7) Indian Water Works Association.

8) National Solid Waste Management Association of India.
9) Institution of Fire Engineers (India).
10) Indian Association of Social Science Associations (IASSI).

Tie-ups with global bodies

The Institute makes exchange of ideas possible to and from institutional global partners. This in turn facilitates new projects, ventures and strategies for urban development schemes. Some of its global partners are as follows-

UNDP, UNCHS, UNICEF, UN-Habitat, US-AEP, WHO, Urban Management Programme (UN-Habitat), GTZ, Germany (German Technical Collaboration), Ford Foundation, British Council, The Canadian International Development Agency, Cities Alliance, Regional Network for Local Authorities for the Management of Human Settlements, Japan (CITYNET), Commonwealth Local Government Forum, International Council for Local Environmental Initiatives (ICLIE), Commonwealth Secretariat, London (UK), Institute of Social Studies (ISS), Netherlands etc.

Ranjit Chavan   **Capt. Anant Modi**
President   **Director General**

Acknowledgements and Gratitude

Global warming and climate change, as the world has come to know, are recent phenomenon, but as a scientific phenomenon climate has been changing since the time the earth has the atmosphere. What is climate change?, how does it take place?, how far it has advanced and affected the earth ecosystem and life?, What potential dangers it has?, etc. are the things explained to the world by the **Intergovernmental Panel on Climate Change (IPCC),** established in 1988, under the auspices of the United Nations. Through its Assessment Reports of its three Working Groups it has unraveled the phenomenon. The **United Nations Framework Convention on Climate Change (UNFCCC)** is a world level body to take action for mitigation and adaption of climate change. **The World Meteorological Organization (WMO)** monitors the world climate with its huge network of technology. Other world level bodies of the **United Nations Environment Programme (UNEP)**, the **Food and Agriculture Organization (FAO), World Health Organization (WHO)** are providing great support services in their respective fields. Thus, it goes without saying that no book on climate change can be written without drawing references to the reports and information sheets of the above world level organization, so generously published and placed on their sites. It is essential for the world not only to know, but to act upon and disseminate the knowledge of climate.

With this view, these bodies have allowed reproduction of limited number of figures or short excerpts free of charge and without formal written permission provided that the original source is properly acknowledged. The UNFCCC has been more generous to place all its material in public domain. The IPCC and the WMO have also kindly given permission for use of images from their publications/sites.

There are other scientific bodies and institutions working on researching and publishing their findings for the world to use. Prominent among them are the **National Aeronautics and Space Administration (NASA) and the National Oceanic and Atmospheric Organization (NOAA).** It is their generosity that they have placed their vast research findings for use, by citing their references. The portals of the **Ministry of Environment and Forests, Government of India, World Resources Institute, World Wildlife Fund, Grid Arendal Publications** etc. make available good deal of knowledge on the subject. **Wikipedia the free encyclopedia** is always there. Besides, there are thousands of institutions that have placed their research work for dissemination of knowledge of climate change.

In his venture to disseminate the knowledge of climate change, the author, while writing this book has drawn references to the vast knowledge resource base of the above high bodies. While doing so utmost care is taken to ensure that scientific facts are taken and references are drawn strictly, as are permitted and by citing the source as required. Thus, the *author acknowledges and expresses deep gratitude* to all the above mentioned bodies- And to the following institutions and organizations.

1. Solar Radiation| Natural Frequency (http://naturalfrequency.com/wiki/solar-radiation.

2. Global Energy Balance (http://www.meteor.iastate.edu/gccourse/alumni/forcing/text.html)

3. Encyclopedia of Earth (www.eoearth.org).

4. Climate Change Wales (www.climatechangewales.org.uk.public).

5. The New Encyclopedia Britannica, 1982.

6. Carbon Budget Fact Sheet-BBC News.

7. Grid Arendal Publications (http://www.grida.no/publictions/vg/climate2/page2648.aspx)

8. Climate Change Evidence (file://D:/Documents and Settings/Administrator/Desktop/Climate Change)

9. CDIAC (http://cdiac.esd.ornl.gov/GCP/carbonbudget/2013/#).

10. Critical Reviews in Plant Sciences 22(5)453-May 2012 (www.tandfoline.com)

11. The Climate System; an Overview (www.grida.no./climate/ipcc/tar/pdf/tar.01)

12. WRI (2005) Navigating the Numbers-Greenhouse Data and International Policy (www.wri.org/publications/navigating the numbers)

13. New World Encyclopedia (www.newworld encyclopedia.org)

14. Times of India, Indian Express, Free Press Journal, daily newspapers issued from Mumbai for their reports relied upon in chapter 18 and Mumbai Mirror for its report in chapter 30.

15. What is CCS? The Carbon Capture and Storage Association (CCSA) (http://www.ccsassociation.org/what –is ccs/)

16. Carbon Capture and Storage Pros and Cons (http://globalwarmingisrael.com/2009/07/16/carbon-capture-and -storage)

17. The Global Status of CCS: February 2014|Global Carbon Capture (http://www.globalccsinstitute. com/publications/global-status-ccs-fe..)

18. Eco-Economy Indicators-Forest Cover| Earth Policy Institute (http://www. Earthpolicy.org/ indicators/C56).

19. Centre for international Forestry Research (CIFOR) and Donato, D et al 2011. Mangroves among the most carbon rich forests in the tropics. Nature Geoscience 45, 293297 as cited in the fact sheet of CIFOR No.5, November,2012-Mitigation (www. cifor.org/fileadmin/factsheet R10+20 Fact Sheet Mitigation.pdf)

20. Commission on the Status of Women (http://www. un.org/womenwatch/daw/csw/57sess.htm)

21. Gender at the Earth Summit, Box 10,Gender equality in the context of climate change (www. un.org/womenwatch/downloads/Resource Guide English-FINAL PDF)

22. Evaluation of Gender Mainstreaming in UNDP (web.undp.org/evaluation/documents/ eogendermainstreaming/pdf)

23. Global Gender and Climate Alliance (http://www. wedo.org/category/themes/sustainable)

24. The World Bank Green Bond Fact Sheet (http://treasury.worldbank.org/cmd/pdf/ WorldBankGreenBondFactSheet.pdf)

25. Petroleum Conservation Research Association(PCRA)(http://www.pcra.org/ English/domestic/lastlong.htm)

26. DBS Bank, Mumbai for citations on its note pad.

27. Ministry of Earth Sciences, Government of India (www.tropmet.res.in/Centre for Climate Change Research.pdf)

28. Indian Meteorological Department. Climate Profile of India. National Communication II by S.D.Attri and Ajit Tyagi, 2010.
29. Planning Commission of India for references taken from the document-Climate Change & 12th Five Year Plan. Report of the Sub-Committee on Climate Change, October, 2011).
30. Ministry of Environment and Forests, Government of India.
31. The Public Diplomacy Division, Ministry of External Affairs.

Chapter 1

GLOBAL WARMING

Photo. 1 Pic Mrs. Purnima Pathak

There are amazing natural phenomena operating on the earth, one of which is an in-built mechanism which keeps the earth warm; warm enough to be habitable and pleasant. Its explanations lay in two things- the energy balance of the earth and the property of certain trace gases, called greenhouse gases, which have a heat trapping property. They absorb and emit heat, called infrared radiation. The global energy balance is the balance between incoming energy from the sun and outgoing heat energy from the earth. However this is not a system of free flow as the outgoing heat is not allowed to go out fully to the outer space. It is held back in the atmosphere to serve a purpose that the nature has designed. Scientists have explained this process. One of the diagrams that are mostly relied upon is the global energy budget, shown as below. Fig. 1.1 (IPCC FAQ 1.1-AR4, WGI[1])

Global Heat Flows

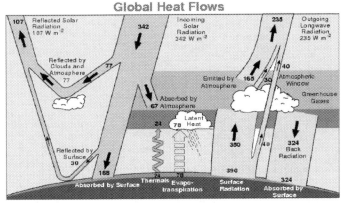

Kiehl and Trenberth 1997

It was prepared by Kiehl, J.T. and Trenberth, K.E. in 1997, which was published in the Bulletin of the American Meteorological Association. Using this diagram, the IPCC in its Fourth Assessment Report have explained the interplay of factors that determine the earth's climate. *Inter alia*, it shows that out of the sun's radiation energy of 1379 watts/sq.meter (w/m²), one fourth of it i.e. 342 w/m² reaches the earth system. After its distribution to various components, reflection, and other use in other processes, about 235 w/m² goes out. While going out, most of it is absorbed by the greenhouses present in the atmosphere[2]. The energy that was received was of various wavelengths, mostly shortwave and ultra-violet, which reached the earth unimpeded, whereas the outgoing is of infrared radiation (i.e. in heat form), for which the greenhouse present in the atmosphere have a propensity to absorb and re-emit. This absorption of outgoing infrared energy (heat) is the natural **greenhouse effect.** This blanketing effect keeps the earth warm and pleasant enough. Had this been not so the earth would have had a temperature around -18⁰C.

Other fundamentals of global climate change related to radiation balance

According to the IPCC, [3] global climate is determined by the radiation balance of the planet. There are three fundamental ways through which the earth's radiation balance can change, thereby causing a climate change:

1) Changing the incoming solar radiation (e.g. by changes in the earth's orbit or in the sun itself),
2) Changing the fraction of solar radiation that is reflected (this fraction is called *albedo*-it can be changed, for example, by changes in cloud cover, small particles called aerosols or land cover), and
3) Altering the long wave energy radiated back to space (e.g.by changes in greenhouse gas concentrations). In addition, local climate also depends on how heat is distributed by winds and ocean currents. All these factors have played a role in the past climate changes."

In the long millions of years of the earth's history, various global climate changes have taken place (explained in another chapter) and there have been ice ages and warm periods. Twenty eight years have passed since the Intergovernmental Panel on Climate Change was set up in 1988. During this period scientists drawn from all over the world, have unraveled the mystery of present warming, by putting the blame on humanity's massive use of fossil fuel, deforestation and other industrial activities, mainly power generation, cement production etc. which generate and continue to generate massive amount of greenhouse gases, namely, carbon dioxide, methane, nitrous oxide etc. which gave rise to **enhanced greenhouse effect.** Following are the broad conclusions which explain present **global warming.**

What is Global Warming?

The United Nations Environment Programme defines global warming as "the recent and ongoing global average increase in temperature near the earth surface" (UNEP – glossary).

The UNFCCC, the apex authority on taking action for adaptation and mitigation, has defined global warming in these words - "An increase in the average temperature of the earth's atmosphere, especially a sustained increase, great enough to cause change in the climate. The present warming is generally attributed to an increase in the greenhouse effect largely due to human industry and agriculture". (UNFCCC glossary of terms).The words 'recent' and 'average surface temperature' need some explanations.

As regards global surface average temperature, the IPCC glossary of terms says – "The global surface temperature is the area-weighted global average of (i) sea surface temperature over the oceans (i.e. the subsurface bulk temperature in the first few meters of the ocean) and (ii) the surface air temperature over land at 1.5 m above the ground.[4]"

In AR4, the IPCC concluded that – "**Expressed as a global average, surface temperatures have increased by 0.74⁰C over the past hundred years (between 1906 and 2005), with most of the warming occurring in the past 50 years**[5].

According to the SPM of AR5[6,] over the period **1880-2012** the globally averaged combined land and ocean surface temperature data, as calculated by a linear trend, show a warming **of 0.85 [0.65 to 1.06]° C**, when multiple independently produced datasets exist. The total increase between the **average of the 1850-1900** period and **2003-2012** period is **0.78 [0.72 to 0.85]° C,** based on the single longest dataset available.

A rise of 0.74 °C or 0.85° C over a hundred years may sound like a small amount. The fact is that this change is in the average surface temperature of the earth, which changes but very slowly and over very long periods, say centuries. The scientists tell us that it is an unusual event in our planet's recent history. The earth's global average temperature remains stable over long periods of time, and small changes in this temperature correspond to enormous changes in the environment[7]

What is the big deal about 1° change in the mean temperature? According to NASA[8], "one degree may sound like a small amount, but it is an unusual event in our planet's recent history. The Earth's climate record, preserved in tree rings, ice cores, and coral reefs, shows that the global average temperature is stable over long periods of time. Furthermore, small changes in temperature correspond to enormous changes in the environment. For example, at the end of the last ice age, when the Northeast United States was covered by more than 3,000 feet of ice, average temperatures were only 5 to 9 degrees cooler than today".

Scientists are suggesting that that the current rate of warming has no parallel within the last thousands of years. The earth's climate is dynamic and changes through natural cycle over a long period. The reason for concern is that the changes that are occurring now have been speeded up because of human activities. According to WMO[9], "Since the beginning of the 20th century, scientists have been observing a change in the climate that cannot be attributed to any of the 'natural' influences of the past only. This change in the climate also known as *global warming* has occurred faster than any other climate change recorded by humans and so is of great interest and importance to the human population."

Causes of Global Warming:

The IPCC, through its thousands of scientists working in its groups, gives its assessments through its reports. Particularly the Fourth Assessment Report (WG I) zeroed in the heat trapping gases, namely carbon dioxide, methane, nitrous oxide, as the main causative factors of global warming. The IPCC compared the relative influence exerted by key heat trapping gases, tiny particles known as aerosols, and land use changes, on our climate system between 1750 and 2005, in the form a graph, that epitomizes their findings.

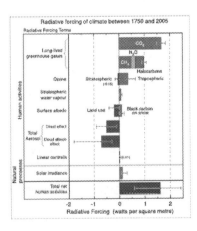

Fig. 1.2 (IPCC,FAQ2.1-AR4 WGI, Chapter 2[10])

Its text says: The values shown in the figure reflect the total forcing relative to the start of the industrial era (about 1750). The forcings for all greenhouse increases, which are the best understood of those due to human activities, are positive because each gas absorbs outgoing infrared radiation in the atmosphere. (*They absorb and re-emit in all directions including downward to the surface*). Among the greenhouse gases, carbon dioxide (CO_2) increases have caused the largest forcing over this period. Tropospheric ozone increases have also contributed to warming, while stratospheric ozone decreases have contributed to cooling.

Aerosol particles influence radiative forcing directly through reflection and absorption of solar and infrared radiation in the atmosphere. Some aerosols cause a positive forcing while others cause a negative forcing. The direct radiative forcing summed over all aerosol types is negative. Aerosols also cause a negative radiative forcing indirectly through the changes they cause in cloud properties. Human activities since the industrial era have altered the nature of land cover over the globe, principally through changes in croplands, pastures and forests. They have also modified the reflective properties of ice and snow. Overall, it is likely that more solar radiation is now being reflected from Earth's surface as a result of human activities. This change results in a negative forcing. The technical term of radiative forcing is explained in the report.

Forcing: Climate varies all the time. The processes, which cause it to change, whether natural or anthropogenic, are known as forcing. Changes in solar radiation are considered to be natural, whereas changes in greenhouse gas concentrations are considered to be anthropogenic. Climate Data Information (www.climatedata.info/forcing/Introduction.html)

What is Radiative Forcing? The influence of a factor that can cause climate change, such as greenhouse gas, is often evaluated in terms of its radiative forcing. Radiative forcing is a measure of how the energy balance of the earth-atmosphere system is influenced when factors that affect climate are altered. The word radiative arises because these factors change the balance between incoming solar radiation and outgoing infrared radiation, with the earth's atmosphere. This radiative balance controls the earth's surface temperature. The term forcing is used to indicate that the earth's radiative balance is pushed away from its normal state. (IPCC)

Box 1

Greenhouse gases

The findings of the IPCC reports lead to the conclusion that these are the greenhouse gases, mainly carbon dioxide, methane and nitrous oxide, which have contributed most to the warming, and among them, contribution of carbon dioxide is the greatest. The following graph clearly bears out the increasing concentration of these gases.

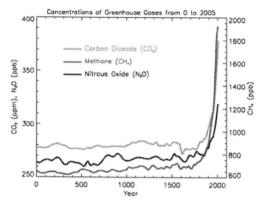

Fig. 1.3 (IPCC AR4,WGI Chapter 2 [11])

The amount of CO_2 in the air increased from the level of 280 parts per million by volume (ppmv) at the pre-industrial to 389 ppmv at the end of 2010. The amount of CO_2 varies throughout the year as the result of the annual cycles of photosynthesis and oxidation. Similarly, methane (CH_4) rose from a pre-industrial atmospheric concentration of around 700 parts per billion by volume (ppbv) to about 1813 ppbv by 2011. Nitrous oxide has risen from the pre-industrial level of 270 ppbv to 324 ppbv in 2011. Of these, carbon dioxide is the single most important gas emitted by human activities is responsible for over 60% of the enhanced greenhouse effect. Current annual emissions amount to over 23 billion metric tons of carbon dioxide[12].

Humanity's greenhouse gas emissions have already disturbed the global energy budget by about 2.5 Watts per square meter. This equals about one percent of the net incoming solar energy that drives the climate system. One per cent may not sound like much, but added up over the earth's entire surface, it amounts to the energy content released by burning 1.8 million tones of oil every minute, or over 100 times the world's current rate of commercial energy consumption. Since greenhouse gases are only a by-product of energy consumption, it is ironic that the amount of energy humanity actually uses are tiny compared to the impact of greenhouse gases on natural energy flows in the climate system[13].

Climate Feedbacks

Greenhouse gases are not alone in their activity. They have supporters or allies in the task of causing warming, what are called *feedbacks*. Changes in one part of the climate system can cause additional changes in the way the planet absorbs or reflects energy. These secondary changes are called *climate feedbacks,* and they could more than double the amount of warming caused by carbon dioxide alone. The primary feedbacks are due to snow and ice, water vapor, clouds, and the carbon cycle. The Fifth Assessment Report of the IPCC 2013-contribution of the Working Group I, further substantiates the findings of its fourth report of 2007, namely[14]:-

"Warming of the climate system in unequivocal, and since the 1950's, many of the observed changes are unprecedented over decades to millennia. The atmosphere and ocean have warmed, the amounts of snow and ice have diminished, the sea levels have risen, and the concentrations of greenhouse gases have increased.

"Human influence has been detected in warming of the atmosphere and the ocean, in changes in the global water cycle, in reductions in snow and ice, in

global mean sea level rise, and in changes in some climate extremes. This evidence for human influence has grown since AR4. It is *extremely likely* that human influence has been the dominant cause of the observed warming since the mid-20th century.

"Continued emissions of green-house gases will cause further warming and changes in all components of the climate system. Limiting climate change will require substantial and sustained reductions of green-house gas emissions."

Global Warming or Climate Change- which term to use?

Global warming and climate change are two different phenomena, the former being a cause of the latter. Hence, they should be used according to the context. Today the concern is of climate change, the dire consequences that have occurred and likely to aggravate. Therefore the IPCC has used this term.

References:

1. IPCC,2007: Climate Change 2007: The Physical Science Basis. Contribution of Working Group I to the Fourth Assessment Report of the Intergovernmental Panel on Climate Change [Solomon.S.,D. Qin, M. Manning, Z. Chen, M. Marquis, K.B. Averyt, M. Tignor and H.L. Miller (eds]. Cambridge University Press, Cambridge, United Kingdom and New York, NY, USA.(FAQ 1.1, Figure 1 –page 96)

2. *Ibid* (FAQ 1.1,Figure 1- page 96)

3. *Ibid*

4. Glossary of terms-Annex B to the IPCC, TAR (www.ipcc.ch/pdf/glossarytar)

5. IPCC 2007:Climate Change *op.cit* (page 253)

6. IPCC Climate Change 2013: *Working Group I- the Physical Science Basis, Summary for Policy Makers.(*IPCC WGI AR5 SPM-2 27 September 2013)(Page 3 SPM)

7. WMO (http//www.int/pages/themes/climatecauses)

8. Climate Change: Effects (http://climate.nasa.gov/effects)

9. WMO (http//www.int/pages/themes/climatecauses)

10. IPCC 2007, *op.cit* (FAQ 2.1 Figure 2-page 136)

11. IPCC 2007, *op.cit* (FAQ 2.1 Figure 1-page 135)

12. WMO Greenhouse Gas Bulletin, November, 2012

13. UNFCCC Climate Change Information Sheet 3 (https://unfccc.int/essential_background/background_publications_ht...)

14. IPCC Climate Change, 2013, *op, cit*

Chapter 2

WEATHER, CLIMATE, CLIMATE SYSTEM AND CLIMATE VARIABILITY

In order to understand climate change, it is necessary to know what the terms 'climate', 'climate system' stand for and the factors which influence them. Hence a brief introduction of these will fit in here.

Photo 2. Pic.
Mr. Nasir Ahmad Khan.

Climate and climate system:

Weather is the topic to break the ice when two persons meet. If they have nothing else to talk, they begin conversation with the weather. It is too hot today! Today winds are blowing so fast, etc. So, weather is what is going on at a particular place *on a particular day and time*. Let us see another set of conversations. I come from a place with a cool climate. The climate of this city is very hot. In this second set of conversations they are talking about the general weather *over a period of time.* This is climate. In this way one can say that climate is an average weather. In these cases we have drawn our inferences very easily. However, this is not so easy when we want to say something about scientific facts. According to IPCC[1]" Climate in the narrow sense is usually defined as the "average weather" or more rigorously as the statistical description in terms of the mean and variability of relevant quantities over a period of time ranging from months to thousands or millions of years. The classical period is 30 years, as defined by the World Meteorological Organization (WMO). These relevant quantities are most often surface variables such as temperature, precipitation and wind. Climate, in a wider sense is the state, including a statistical description, of the climate system".

Climate consists of various factors. These are called *variables*, because they go on varying. They affect the daily life directly. Broadly, these are: average, maximum and minimum temperature, wind near the surface of the earth, atmospheric pressure, precipitation, humidity, cloud type and amount, and solar radiation etc. There are as many as 26 variables.

Climate of a region is generated by the climate system. Climates are determined by many factors, which include latitude, topography, distance from the sea, location of the continent etc. Geography texts explain these facts lucidly. For example places that lie on or near equator have a tropical climate As this region receives substantial sun heat it causes water to evaporate and form clouds. As such, this region has a hot and humid climate. Places farther from the equator have temperate climate. The USA, Europe, China, Russia, South America etc. They have typical four seasons. As for example of the influence of the factors - north and south of the equator the trade winds blow from the northeast and southeast respectively. These winds converge in the tropics, forcing air to rise. This produces thunderstorms, humidity, and the monsoons. North and south of trade winds, about 30^0 from the equator, there is relatively little wind, and therefore little moisture blowing inland from the oceans. Also, dry air sinks back to the surface, getting warm in the process. This is why many of the world's great desert regions- the Sahara, Arabia, Iraq, and many parts of Mexico lie at the same latitude. Mountains force wind to rise as it crosses over them. This cools the air, causing moisture to condense in clouds and rain. This produces a wet climate on the upwind wide of the mountains and arid 'rain shadow' on the downwind side. Oceans provide moisture and buffer temperature of coastal regions, regardless of latitude[2].

According to IPCC [3] "Climate system is an interactive system consisting of five major components: the atmosphere, the hydrosphere, cryosphere, the land surface and the biosphere, forced or influenced by various external forcing mechanisms, the most important of which is the sun. Also, the direct effect of human activities on climate system is considered an external forcing."

According to WMO, [4] "In a broader sense, climate is the status of the climate system, which comprises the hydrosphere, the cryosphere, the surface lithosphere and the biosphere. These elements determine the state of dynamics of the earth's climate. The atmosphere is the envelope of gases surrounding the earth."

Hydrosphere is a part of the climate system containing liquid water at the earth's surface and underground (e.g. ocean, rivers, and lakes)

Cryosphere contains water in its frozen state (i.e. glaciers, snow, ice, etc.)

Surface lithosphere is the upper layer of solid earth on land and oceans supporting volcanic activity which influence climate.

Biosphere contains all living organisms and ecosystems over the land and in the oceans.

Climate Variability

Literally speaking, the words 'change' and 'variability' look similar. In the context of climate change science both are different and care must be taken not to confuse one with the other. We often read or hear that a particular day was the hottest or a particular night was the coldest in so many years. This determination is with reference to some mean or what is taken as normal. Mean is determined on the basis of 30 years' climate data. Extreme event is one that occurs once in 30 years. Apart from extreme events there are some deviations from the 'normal' at any point of time. An example will make it clear. Mumbai's average rainfall per year is 242 cm. However, there could be no year when the actual rainfall was 242 cm. If ten years actual rainfall is drawn on a chart it will give a zigzag picture. This variation from the mean or average is variability.

Variables of climate are continuously recorded. A mean is arrived at of this statistical record for a definite period of time of ten years and thirty years. Climate is dynamic and keeps on varying every hour, every day. Any deviation from this mean is climate variability. This may be due to natural internal processes within the climate system or to variations in natural anthropogenic external forcing. The UNFCCC in its Article 1 makes this clear as it defines 'climate change' as "a change of climate which is attributed directly or indirectly to human activities that alter the composition of the global atmosphere and which is in addition to natural climate variability observed over comparable time periods.

References:

1. Glossary of Terms-Annex B to TAR (www.ipcc.ch/pdg/glossary/tar)

2. Climate, Climate Information, Facts-National Geography (http://science.nationalgeographic.co.in/science/earth/earth's atmosphere)

3. Climate System: an Overview (chapter) IPCC Third Assessment Report(www.grida.no/climate/ipcc-tar/pdf/tar .01)

4. WMO (FAQs) (www.wmo.int/pages / PWO / WCP / CLE / Faqs)

Chapter 3

CLIMATE CHANGE

Photo 3. Pic. Mr. Ramesh Patil.

The climate of the earth has been changing since the time the earth has atmosphere. Over the millions of years of earth's history *"climate on Earth has changed on all time-scales, including long before human activity could have a role[1]"*. Climate change on the earth is an old phenomenon because "Global climates are influenced by incoming solar radiation, the arrangement of landmasses and water bodies, and composition of the atmosphere. These conditions, and therefore climate, can change over time. Paleoclimatic data indicates that the Earth has experienced both warm phases and ice ages, with the cold phases lasting generally for shorter periods. In the mid cretaceous period (120 to 90 million years ago), dinosaurs roamed in northern areas and sea-levels were much higher than at present, as less water was held as ice. The most recent geological period, the Quaternary, has seen numerous oscillations in temperature and ice caps. The earth is at present in Holocene period, which began about 15 thousand years ago. The warming was interrupted by a cold phase called the Younger Dryas, but about 11,800 years ago an abrupt warming brought the climate into the interglacial phase we are experiencing today[2]".

This chapter begins with the above two quotations from the highest scientific authorities- the IPCC and WMO, to drive home the point that as per the scheme of the things of nature, climate change is a normal part of the Earth's natural variability, as the atmosphere, oceans, land and the changes in the amount of solar radiation are made to always interact with each other, and as a result thereof the climate, by its very nature, is made to change. *What is new* to the climate change that has been experienced since about the last three decades, taken as a concern, researched, studied, documented and declared as a threat, as found out, is that *it is caused by human hand and it is proceeding at a rate that is unprecedented in the past.* Scientists from most of the countries were made to work together (IPCC), all the available technology was made to use, climate data from all the countries gathered and the scientists could see the big picture that this time warming trend and consequent climate change is human-induced and caused by the gases called *greenhouse gases.* In these vast studies the heat trapping property of these gases was recalled to record (nature created these trace gases for the same purpose, to keep the earth warm enough to be habitable, as we shall see in the book), concentrations of these gases at the time of the first Industrial Revolution (1750) and the second Industrial Revolution (1850) were taken as a benchmark, and it was found that the global abundance of carbon dioxide (CO_2) increased by 40% relative to 1750; that of methane (CH_4) by 159% and nitrous oxide 20%. The last three decades have been very eye opening for the humanity, when the IPCC, through its Assessment Reports (1990.1992.1996.2001,2007,2013 and 2014) unraveled the whole story. Its latest report AR5 /WGI,2013[3] says:

1. Warming of the climate system is unequivocal, and since the 1950s, many of the observed changes are unprecedented over decades to millennia. The atmosphere and ocean have warmed, the amounts of snow and ice have diminished, sea level has risen, and the concentrations of greenhouse gases have increased

2. The atmospheric concentrations of carbon dioxide, methane, and nitrous oxide have increased to levels unprecedented in at least the last 800,000 years. Carbon dioxide concentrations have increased by 40% since pre-industrial times, primarily from fossil fuel emissions and secondarily from net land use change emissions. The ocean has absorbed about 30% of the emitted anthropogenic carbon dioxide, causing ocean acidification

3. Human influence on the climate system is clear. This is evident from the increasing greenhouse gas concentrations in the atmosphere, positive radiative forcing, observed warming, and understanding of the climate system

With this background we shall discuss climate change.

Climate change - definition:

According to the glossary of terms used in the IPCC Fourth Assessment Report (WGI) [4] "Climate change refers to a change in the state of the *climate* that can be identified (e.g.

by using statistical tests) by changes in the mean and/or the variability of its properties and that persists for an extended period, typically decades or longer. Climate change may be due to natural internal processes or *external forcings* or to persistent anthropogenic changes in the composition of the *atmosphere* or in *land use*. Note that the United Nations *Framework Convention on Climate Change* (UNFCCC), in its Article 1, defines: climate **change** as: "a change of climate which is attributed directly or indirectly to human activity that alters the composition of the global atmosphere and which is in addition to natural climate variability observed over comparable time periods". The UNFCCC thus makes a distinction between climate change attributable to human activities altering the atmospheric composition and *climate variability* attributable to natural causes."

(*External forcing refers to a forcing agent outside the climate system causing a change in the climate system. Volcanic eruptions, solar variations and anthropogenic changes in the composition of the atmosphere and land use changed are external forcing – (ibid Glossary)*

Causes of Climate Change:

According to IPCC[5"] Global climate is determined by the radiation balance of the planet. There are three fundamental ways the earth's radiation balance can change, thereby causing a climate change:

1) Changing the incoming solar radiation (e.g. by changes in the earth's orbit or in the sun itself),
2) Changing the fraction of solar radiation that is reflected (this fraction is called *albedo*-it can be

changed, for example, by changes in cloud cover, small particles called aerosols or land cover), and

3) Altering the long wave energy radiated back to space (e.g.by changes in greenhouse gas concentrations). In addition, local climate also depends on how heat is distributed by winds and ocean currents. All these factors have played a role in the past climate changes."

In the present times the third cause has become of significance as stated above.

The World Meteorological Organization notes three major causes of climate change [6:]

❖ Greenhouse gases
❖ Aerosols
❖ Land use change

Greenhouse gases: The ultimate source of energy that drives the climate system is radiation from the sun. First, greenhouse gases let the visible and ultraviolet light (its dangerous part is blocked by ozone layer) in sunlight to pass through Earth's atmosphere to reach the Earth's surface. This solar energy is absorbed by the clouds, the atmosphere and the earth surface; where it is transformed to heat energy. This absorbed energy raises the surface temperature and also evaporates surface water to create atmospheric water vapour. The earth, compared with outer space is very warm. It must therefore release energy to maintain the balance. Since it has energy in the form of heat (infrared) it radiates back the heat, which is partly absorbed by the greenhouse gases present in the atmosphere and a part of it escapes to space. The heat absorbed by the greenhouses is retained and re-emitted to the earth. **This is greenhouse effect**[7], which is the crux of the matter. Now that the concentrations of greenhouse gases have increased considerably, they are absorbing, retaining and re-emitting more heat raising the global mean temperature, causing *enhanced greenhouse effect*. Thus, the greenhouse gases act like a blanket to keep the earth warm. These gases comprise less than 1% of the atmosphere.

The main greenhouse gases include (i) water vapour, (ii) carbon dioxide (CO_2), (iii) methane (CH_4), (iv) nitrous oxide (N_2O) and (v) chlorofluorocarbon. Since the beginning of the 20th century industrial activity grew 40 fold and the emissions of greenhouse gas grew 10 fold.

The amount of CO_2 in the air increased from the level of 280 parts per million by volume (ppmv) at the pre-industrial level to 389 ppmv at the end of 2010. The amount of CO_2 varies throughout the year as the result of the annual cycles of photosynthesis and oxidation. Similarly, methane (CH_4) rose from a pre-industrial atmospheric concentration of around 700 parts per billion by volume (ppbv) to about 1813 ppbv by 2011. Nitrous oxide has risen from the pre-industrial level of 270 ppbv to 324 ppbv in 2011[8.] Of these carbon dioxide is the single most important gas emitted by human activities is responsible for over 60% of the enhanced greenhouse effect. Current annual emissions amount to over 23 billion metric tons of carbon dioxide[9].

Water vapour is the most abundant heat-trapping gas, but rarely discussed when considering human-induced climate change. Nevertheless, water vapour matters for climate change because of an important "positive feedback".

Warmer air can hold more moisture, and models predict that a small global warming would lead to a rise in global water vapour levels, further adding to the enhanced greenhouse effect[10].

"The overall warming from 1850 to the end of the 20th century was equivalent to about 2.5 W/m^2; CO_2 contributed around 60 per cent of this figure and CH_4 about 25 per cent, while N_2O and halocarbons providing the remainder. This has resulted in increase in the Earth's average temperature from 15.5°C to 16.2°C in the last 100 years. The warming effect that would result from a doubling of CO2 from pre-industrial levels is estimated to be 4 W/m^2." [11]

Aerosols in the Atmosphere

Aerosoles are a collection of airborne solid or liquid particles, with a typical size between 0.01 and 10mm that reside in the atmosphere for at least several hours. Aerosoles may be of either natural or anthropogenic origin.

"Atmospheric aerosols are able to alter climate in two important ways:

1. They scatter and absorb solar and infrared radiation.
2. They may change the microphysical and chemical properties of clouds and possibly their lifetime and extent.

The scattering of solar radiation acts to cool the planet, while absorption of solar radiation by aerosols warms the air directly instead of allowing sunlight to be absorbed by the surface of the Earth.

- Human activity contributes to the amount of aerosols in the atmosphere in several ways.
- Dust is often a bi-product of agricultural processes.
- Biomass burning produces a combination of organic droplets and soot particles.
- Industrial processes produce a wide variety of aerosols depending on what is being burned or produced in the manufacturing process.
- Exhaust emissions from transport generate a rich cocktail of pollutants that are either aerosols from the outset, or are converted by chemical reactions in the atmosphere to form aerosols.

The concentrations of aerosols are about three times higher in the northern hemisphere than in the southern hemisphere. This higher concentration is estimated to result in radiation forcing that is about 50 per cent higher in the northern hemisphere. "[12]

Land use, land-use change and forestry

According to the UNFCCC[13] deforestation is the second largest source of carbon dioxide." When forests are cleared for agriculture or development, most of the carbon in the burned or decomposing trees escapes to the atmosphere. However, when new forests are planted the growing trees absorb carbon dioxide, removing it from the atmosphere. Recent net deforestation has occurred mainly in the tropics. There is a great deal of scientific uncertainty about emissions from deforestation and other land-use changes, but it is estimated that from 800 million to 2.4 billion tonnes of carbon are released globally every year.[13]" The IPCC AR4 has estimated that deforestation and forest degradation contribute globally 17% of greenhouse gas contribution.

"Land-use changes (e.g. cutting down forests to create farmland) have led to changes in the amount of sunlight reflected from the ground back into space (the surface albedo). The scale of these changes is estimated to be about one-fifth of the forcing on the global climate due to changes in emissions of greenhouse gases. About half of the land use changes are estimated to have occurred during the industrial era, much of it due to replacement of forests by agricultural cropping and grazing lands over Eurasia and North America." [14]

(The mechanism of the greenhouse effect and the sources, concentrations of greenhouse gases are explained in detail in the respective chapters)

Summing Up:

So, the bottomline is that changes in the statistics of the weather (its variables) have taken place that have altered the composition of the global atmosphere, which are in addition to natural variability and are attributed directly or indirectly to human activity, and that these are detrimental to the ecosystems of the earth and thus to life on the earth. Thus, the words 'climate change' are now not used in their generic scientific sense but as specific for the present times that are caused by human hand and are of long-term nature, and need to be addressed with all the seriousness and urgency.

References:

1. IPCC,2007:Climate Change, 2007:: *The Physical Science Basis Working Group I Contribution to Fourth Assessment Report of the Intergovernmental Panel on Climate Change*:[Solomon, Susan. Qin, Dahe. Manning, Martin. Marquis, Melinda. Averyt, Kristen. Tignor, Melinda M.B. Miller. Henry Le Roy, Jr. Chen, Zhenlin. (eds.)] Cambridge University Press, Cambridge, United Kingdom and New York, NY, USA. (FAQ 6.1-page 449)

2. WMO 50-Global Climate (http://www.wmo.int/pages/ about/wmo50/e/world/climate_e.html)

3. Summary for Policymakers of the Fifth Assessment Report of IPCC-Contribution of the Working Group I Pages 4,11,15) (https://www.ipcc.ch/report/ar5/ wg1/docs/WGIAR5_SPM_brochure_en.pdf)

4. IPCC 2007,*op.cit* (page 943)

5. IPCC 2007 (FAQ 1.1),*op.cit* (page 96)

6. WMO – Causes of Climate Change (www.wmo.int/ pages/themes/climate/causes_of_climate_change.php)

7. Global Energy Balance (http://www.meteor.iastate. edu/gccourse/alumni/forcing/text.html)

8. WMO Greenhouse Gas Bulletin November, 2012.

9. UNFCCC Climate Change Information Sheet 3 (http://unfccc.int/essential_background/ background_publications_ht..)

10. *Ibid*

11. WMO Causes of Climate Change, *op.cit*

12. WMO Causes of Climate Change, *op.cit*

13. UNFCCC Climate Change Information Sheet, *op.cit*

14. WMO- Causes of Climate Change, *op.cit*

Chapter 4

HISTORY OF PAST CLIMATE CHANGES

And the earth was waste and void- Genesis 1.

In the long history of the earth whether climate changes have taken place?

What have been the causes?

How is today's warming different from the past?

"Climate on Earth has changed on all time scales, including long before human activity could have played a role. Great progress has been made in understanding the causes and mechanisms of these climate changes. Changes in Earth's radiation balance were the principal driver of past climate changes, but the causes of such changes are varied. For each case – be it the Ice Ages, the warmth at the time of the dinosaurs or the fluctuations of the past millennium – the specific causes must be established individually. In many cases, this can now be done with good confidence, and many past climate changes can be reproduced with quantitative models[1]"

The earth has a history of about 4,500 million years. We get amazing information from the science, lucidly presented in atlases, that in the beginning there was a whirling globe of stellar gas. Then the earth passed through a liquid state before a solidified crust was formed. The earth passed through many major disturbances of its crust, which caused important changes in the geography and climate. Based on these changes the geological history is drawn into four separate *eras* and 16 *periods*. The geologists have unearthed these changes through the evidence they found in the rocks and in the fossilized relics of plants and animals. And paleoclimatologists, through examining rocks, sediments, ice sheets, tree rings, corals, shells and microfossils have found the past states of the earth's climate.

Based on all these vast information, the scientists have now a definite picture of the past climates, and how they changed in the past. Most of the scientific findings in respect of climate change have now seal of approval of the IPCC. According to IPCC [2"] Global climate is determined by the radiation balance of the planet. There are three fundamental ways the earth's radiation balance can change, thereby causing a climate change:

1) Changing the incoming solar radiation (e.g. by changes in the earth's orbit or in the sun itself);

2) changing the fraction of solar radiation that is reflected (this fraction is called *albedo*-it can be changed, for example, by changes in cloud cover, small particles called aerosols or land cover), and

3) altering the long wave energy radiated back to space (e.g.by changes in greenhouse gas concentrations). In addition, local climate also

depends on how heat is distributed by winds and ocean currents. All these factors have played a role in the past climate changes."

Ice ages

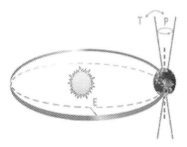

Milankovitch Cycles. Schematic of the Earth's orbital changes (Milankovitch cycles) that drive the ice age cycles. 'T' denotes changes in the tilt (or obliquity) of the Earth's axis, 'E' denotes changes in the eccentricity of the orbit (due to variations in the minor axis of the ellipse), and 'P' denotes precession, that is, changes in the direction of the axis tilt at a given point of the orbit. Source: Rahmstorf and Schelinhuber (2006)

Fig. 4.1 (IPCC AR4 WGI, FAQ 6.1-page 449)

Image of Milankovitch given in IPCC AR4,WGI, Chapter 6. IPCC has sourced this image from Rahmstorf and Schelinhuber (2006)

Ice ages have occurred in regular cycles in the last three million years. Scientists have shown that they are linked to regular variations in the earth's orbit around the sun. They are called Milankovitch cycles. These cycles change the amount of solar radiation received at each latitude in each season, though they may not have effect on global mean. Many studies have pointed out that the amount of summer sunshine on northern continents is crucial: if it drops below a critical value, snow from the past does not melt away in summer and ice sheet starts to grow as snow accumulates. Climate simulations have confirmed ice age can be started this way. Scientists have also used conceptual models to show how past glacial changes have occurred based on orbital changes. The next large reduction in northern summer insolation, similar to those that started past Ice Ages, is due to begin in 30,000 years[3].

Role of carbon dioxide

The scientific findings have also established the key role of carbon dioxide in the ice ages. Antarctic ice core data show that CO_2 concentration is low in the cold glacial times (~190 ppm), and high in the warm interglacials (~280ppm); atmosphericCO_2 follows temperature changes in Antarctica with a lag of some hundreds of years. Because the climate changes at the beginning and end of ice ages take several thousand years, most of these changes are affected by a positive CO_2 feedback; that is, a small initial cooling due to the Milankovitch cycles is subsequently amplified as the CO_2 concentration falls. Model simulations of ice age climate yield realistic results only if the role of CO_2 is accounted for[4].

There is correlation between the levels of carbon dioxide and the temperature.

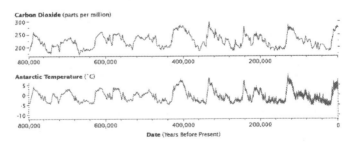

Fig.4.2 Image: courtesy-The Carbon Cycle: Feature Articles (http://earthobservatory.nasa.gov/Features/CarbonCycle/Page4.php)

During the last ice age, over 20 abrupt and dramatic climate shifts occurred that are particularly prominent in records around the northern Atlantic. These differ from the glacial-interglacial cycles in that they probably do not involve large changes in global mean temperature: changes are not synchronous in Greenland and Antarctica, and they are in the opposite direction in the South and North Atlantic. This means that a major change in global radiation balance would not have been needed to cause these shifts; a redistribution of heat within the climate system would have sufficed. There is indeed strong evidence that changes in ocean circulation and heat transport can explain many features of these abrupt events; sediment data and model simulations show that some of these changes could have been triggered by instabilities in the ice sheets surrounding he Atlantic at the time, and the associate freshwater release into the ocean[5].

Warmer periods

As ice ages have occurred, similarly warmer times have also occurred in climate history, during the most of the past 500 million years, Geologists have studied ice marks on rock to conclude that Earth was probably completely free of ice sheets, during such warmer periods, unlike today, when Greenland and Antarctica are ice-covered. Data on greenhouse gas abundances going back beyond a million years, that is, beyond the reach of Antarctic ice cores, are still uncertain, but analysis of geological samples suggests that the warm ice-free periods coincide with high atmospheric CO2 levels. On million-year time scales, CO2 levels change due to tectonic activity, which affects the rates of CO2 exchange of ocean and atmosphere with the solid Earth[6].

Solar Output

Variations in the energy output of the Sun are another likely cause of past climatic changes. Measurements over recent decades show that the solar output varies slightly (by close to 0.1%) in an 11 year cycle. Sunspot observations (going back to the 17th century), as data from isotopes generated by cosmic radiation, provide evidence for longer-term changes in solar activity. Data correlation and model simulations indicate that solar variability and volcanic activity are likely to be leading reasons for climate variations during past millennium, before the start of the industrial era[7]. These examples illustrate that different climate changes in the past had different causes.

Paleoclimatic research has unearthed a great deal of the climatic conditions of the past, which have been variously cited by various scientific authorities. Paleoclimatic data indicates that the earth has experienced both warm phases and ice ages, with the cold phases lasting generally for shorter periods. "In the mid cretaceous period (120 to 90 million years ago), dinosaurs roamed in northern areas and sea levels were much higher than at present, as less water was held as ice. The most recent geological period, the Quarternary, has seen numerous oscillations in temperature and ice caps. These are called glacial/interglacial cycles. The earth is at present in the Holocene period, which began about 15 thousand years ago. The warming was interrupted by a cold phase called the Younger Dryas, but about 11,800 years ago, an abrupt warming brought the climate into the interglacial phase we are experiencing today[8]".

Thus, we are fortunate that some 10,000 years ago, the ice age ended. In the warm period that ensued from then man developed agriculture, civilization, industry and technology in a global climate which has been warm, pleasant and most predictable[9]. Various scientific inventions and discoveries, age of Renaissance, first Industrial Revolution (1750), the second Industrial Revolution (1850), great explorations of the earth, discovery of fossil fuels and means of turning energy trapped within them into heat, transportation, development of manufacturing and constructions etc. have tremendously transformed the human life and human activities. However, this modern life and way of doing things produced a side effect of increase in the concentrations of carbon dioxide, methane and nitrous oxide –the greenhouse gases which enhanced the natural greenhouse effect and the phenomenon we known as *global warming* and *climate change* ensued.

From the second half of the 20th century, a series of aberrations of climatic events, scientific findings of the possible effects of greenhouse gases, deliberations of World Climate Conferences, led the World Meteorological Organization (WMO) and the United Nations Environment Programme (UNEP) to form a scientific body namely the Intergovernmental Panel on Climate Change (IPCC) in 1988, to *assess the state of existing knowledge about climate change; its science, the environmental, economic and social impacts and possible response strategies*. From then, there has been a spate of research the world over on climate science, world climate and climate change. The IPCC has been assessing all these vast findings and data and coming out with its authentic versions through its Assessment Reports. It has been established that in the 20th century, the influence of human activities, burning fossil fuels, deforestation, and similar activities have change the chemical composition of the atmosphere, which has impacted the natural system. The increasing concentrations of carbon dioxide and other greenhouse gases in the atmosphere enhance the natural greenhouse effect, leading to increase in the earth's average surface temperature, sea level and weather patterns, which will dramatically change the earth. It is now a confirmed fact that **Human influence has been detected in warming of the atmosphere and the ocean, in changes in the global water cycle, in reductions in snow and ice, in global mean sea level rise, and in changes in some climate extremes. This evidence for human influence has grown since AR4. It is *extremely likely* that human influence has been the dominant cause of the observed warming since the mid-20th century[10].**

References:

1. FAQ 6.1, IPCC 2007: Climate Change 2007: The Physical Science Basis. Contribution of Working Group I to the Fourth Assessment Report of the Intergovernmental Panel on Climate Change [Solomon, S., D. Qin, M. Manning, Z. Chen, M. Marquis, K.B. Averyt, M.Tignor and H.L. Miller (eds.)]. Cambridge University Press, Cambridge, United Kingdom and New York, NY, USA. FAQ 6.2-page 465)

2. *Ibid* (FAQ 1.1-page 96)

3. *Ibid* (FAQ 6.1 page 449)

4. *Ibid* (FAQ 6.1 page 449)

5. *Ibid* (FAQ 6 -page 449)

6. *Ibid* (FAQ 6.1 page 449)

7. *Ibid* (FAQ 6.1 page 450)

8. WMO 50-Global Climate (http://www.wmo.int/pages/about/wmo50/e/world/climate_e.html)

9. Global Climate Change: Background Material (http://www.ucar.edu/learn/1_4_1.htm)

10. (IPCC Fifth Assessment Report, Working Group I –the Physical Science Basis-SummaryReportSeptember,2013.(https://www.ipcc.ch/report/ar5/wg1/docs/WGIAR5_SPM_brochure_en.p)(page 15)

Chapter 5

GREENHOUSE EFFECT

The greenhouse effect is the crux of the matter for causing atmospheric warming effect and consequently the climate change. If one has understood greenhouse effect, one has understood global warming. Just as a greenhouse is made to retain the heat, nature has provided the mechanism of the greenhouse effect to keep the atmosphere of the earth warm enough, so that a lot of processes and cycles go on, and life is sustained.

Greenhouse: A greenhouse (also called glass house) is a structure in which vegetables, flowers and plants are grown. It is a covered structure having roof and walls of glass. It allows for greater control over the inside environment, temperature, shade etc. In cooler countries and in winter it is more useful as it keeps the warmth inside by trapping the heat. The green house gets warmed because incoming visible solar radiation (glasses being transparent) from the sunlight is absorbed by plants, soil and other things inside the structure. The air, warmed by the heat from hot interior surface, is retained in the structure by the roof and the walls. In addition, the warmed structures and plants inside the greenhouse re-radiate some of their thermal energy in the infra-red spectrum, to which glass is partly opaque, so some of this energy is trapped inside the glasshouse. However this latter process is a minor player compared with the former (convective) process. Thus, the primary heating mechanism is convection. In this way glass used for a greenhouse works as a barrier to air flow and its effect is to trap energy within the greenhouse.

Greenhouse Effect

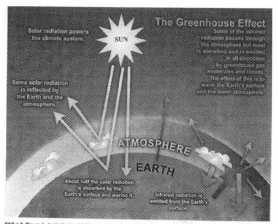

FAQ 1.3, Figure 1. An idealised model of the natural greenhouse effect. See text for explanation.

Fig. 5.1 (IPCC FAQ 1.3 AR4, WG1)[1]

The greenhouse effect is a built-in mechanism designed by nature in the interest of the inhabitants of the earth. This is how it works-

The earth receives energy from the sun, mostly in the form of visible radiation.

1. Some solar radiation is reflected by the earth, the atmosphere and the clouds.

2. About half of the solar radiation is absorbed by the earth's surface.

3. Absorbed by land, oceans and vegetation at the surface, the visible light is transformed into heat.

4. When energy is absorbed by any substance, it raises its temperature (in this case, of the atmosphere and the surface of the planet). Thus, surface temperature rises. In case of water on the surface, this raised temperature causes water to evaporate, which creates atmospheric water.

5. If an object is heated, i.e. when it has a temperature higher than its surroundings, then it loses energy to its surrounding by infrared radiation (this is a technical term for heat). From day to day life, we see that when a stove is put off, its burner is very hot. However, it begins to lose heat, and after sometimes it acquires the temperature of the room. The earth, as a result of receiving solar radiation and that solar radiation having been transformed into heat, the earth, compared to the outer space becomes very warm. So, it radiates energy in the infrared form, a rate that is proportional to the fourth power of the temperature (this is scientific principle).

6. If this would have continued without any obstruction, then, like the example of the burner of the stove, the earth should become very cold in the night.

7. But here is the catch! There is big obstruction in the way of flow of this infrared radiation given off by the earth. There are molecules of some gases, called greenhouse gases in the atmosphere, which have a propensity of absorbing this infrared energy. They absorb most of this out going infrared radiation, and

keep on re-emitting it in all directions, including downward. Only some of the infrared radiation manages to escape to outer space. Thus, infrared radiation, i.e. heat is retained in the atmosphere; it keeps on circulation, as if there is a blanket. This blanketing of heat, its absorption by greenhouse gases and re-emitting is **the greenhouse effect.** Because of this greenhouse effect, earth's average temperature is warm enough to be habitable and water goes on with its cycle. Had this not been so the earth would have had average temperature of about -18^0 C. (Please see similar explanation of greenhouse effect, in quantifying terms of energy, in the chapter on global warming)

IPCC's version[2]:

*"The sun powers the earth's climate, radiating energy at very short wavelengths, predominately in the visible or near-visible (e.g., ultraviolet) part of the spectrum. Roughly one-third of the solar energy that reaches the top of the earth's atmosphere is reflected directly back to space. The remaining two-thirds are absorbed by the surface and, to a lesser extent, by the atmosphere. To balance the absorbed incoming energy, the earth must, on average, radiate almost the same amount of energy back to the space. Because the earth is much cooler than the sun, it radiates at much longer wavelengths, primarily in the infrared part of the spectrum. Much of this thermal radiation emitted by the land and ocean is absorbed by the atmosphere by greenhouse gases in the atmosphere, including clouds, and reradiated back to the earth. This is called **the greenhouse effect.** The glass walls in a greenhouse reduce airflow and increase the temperature*

of the air inside. Analogously, but through a different physical process, the Earth's greenhouse effect warms the surface of the planet. Without the natural greenhouse effect, the average temperature at Earth's surface would be below the freezing point of water. Thus, Earth's greenhouse effect makes, as we know it possible. However, human activities, primarily the burning of fossil fuels and clearing of forests, have greatly intensified the natural greenhouse effect, causing global warming".

While the natural greenhouse effect is a boon to the inhabitants of the earth, this boon is now becoming a bane. What is of concern is the **enhanced greenhouse effect** caused by increasing concentrations of greenhouse gases in the atmosphere, due to human activity on account of massive fossil fuel burning, deforestation, industrial processes, land use and biomass burning, etc. Simply put, the thicker the blanket of greenhouse gases, the more heat is retained by it and greenhouse effect is enhanced. According to the IPCC- "An increase in the concentration of greenhouse gases leads to an increased infrared opacity of the atmosphere, and therefore to an effective radiation into space from a higher altitude at a lower temperature. This causes a *radiative forcing*, an imbalance that can only be compensated for by an increase of the temperature of the surface-troposphere system. This is the "**enhanced greenhouse effect**.[3]"

Increased concentrations of greenhouse gases are discussed in the next chapter. However, in the context of the enhanced greenhouse effect, a few broad facts are mentioned here.

- Largest contributor to the natural greenhouse effect is water vapour. Its presence in the atmosphere is directly affected by human activity. Nevertheless, water vapour matters for climate change because of an important 'positive feedback'. Warmer air can hold more moisture, and models predict that a small global warming would lead to a rise on global water vapour levels, further adding to the enhanced greenhouse effect[4].

- Carbon dioxide is currently responsible for over 60% of the enhanced greenhouse effect. This gas occurs naturally in the atmosphere, but burning coal, oil, and natural gas is releasing the carbon stored in this fossil fuel at an unprecedented rate. Likewise, deforestation releases carbon stored in trees. Current annual emissions amount to over 23 billion metric tons of carbon dioxide[5].

- Methane from past emissions currently contributes 20% of the enhanced greenhouse effect. The rapid rise in methane started more recently than the rise in carbon dioxide, but methane's contribution has been catching up fast. However, methane has an effective atmospheric lifetime of only 12 years, whereas carbon dioxide survives much longer[6].

- Nitrous oxide, a number of industrial gases, and ozone contribute the remaining 20% of the enhanced greenhouse effect[7].

How long do we know natural greenhouse effect?

The IPCC, in its First Assessment Report (1990) stated that *"We are certain that there is a natural greenhouse effect.... resulting from human activities is substantially increasing the atmosphere concentrations of the greenhouse gases."*

It was French polymath Jean-Baptiste Fourier who had first predicted in 1827 that an atmospheric effect keeps the earth warmer than it would otherwise be. He was the first scientist to use a greenhouse analogy. In 1860s, physicist John Tyndall recognized the Earth's natural greenhouse effect and suggested that slight changes in the atmospheric composition could bring about climatic variations. In 1896, a seminal paper by Swedish scientist Svante Arrhenius first speculated that changes in the levels of carbon dioxide in the atmosphere could substantially alter the surface temperature through the greenhouse effect[8]. Atmospheric scientists first used the term 'greenhouse effect' in the early 1880s. At that time, it was used to describe the naturally occurring functions of trace gases in the atmosphere and did not have any negative connotations. It was not until 1950s that the term greenhouse effect was coupled with concern over climate change. Today it is the buzzword.

During the 1890s Swedish scientist Svante Arrhenius and an American P.C. Chamberlain, independently considered the problems that might be caused by CO_2 building up in the atmosphere. Both scientists realized that the burning of fossil fuel could lead to global warming, but neither suspected the process might have already begun[9].

Greenhouse effect and its relation to climate change[10]

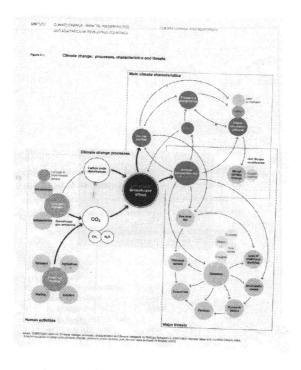

Fig. 5.2 Reference; UNEP/GRID-Arendal. Permission to use material from GRID Arendal (http://www.grida.no/general/2832.aspx)

The illustration shown in the graphic is the key to why the boon of greenhouse effect has become a bane in its enhanced form. Because, it sets off a chain of reactions which is best illustrated in a graphic by UNEP/GRID Adernal[13].

The above graph shows the chains of reaction:

1. First chain of actions led to the greenhouse effect taking place.
2. This sets off a chain of reactions- temperature rise, melting of ice caps, water evaporation, cloud formation, precipitation, salinity, oceans upheavels, abrupt climate change, gulf stream modification, europe cooling.
3. Third set of reactions are set of impacts that we are grappling with. These are disasters, sea-level rise, spread of diseases, casualties, famines, economic losses, loss of traditional lifestyles, droughts, heat waves, floods, cyclones

References:

1. IPCC, 2007: Climate Change 2007.: The Physical Science Basis:: Contribution of Working Group I to the Fourth Assessment Report of the Intergovernmental Panel on Climate Change [Solomon, S., D.Qin, M.Manning, Z.Chen, M.Marquis. K.B. Averyt, M.Tignor and H.L. Miller (eds.)].Cambridge University Press, Cambridge, United Kingdom and New York, NY, USA. (FAQ 1.3 page 115)

2. *ibid*

3. Glossary of Terms – Annex B to the IPCC, Third Assessment Report (www.ipcc.ch/pdf/glossary/tar)

4. IPCC 2007:Climate Change 2007, *op.cit*

5. Climate Change Information Sheet (http://unfccc.int/ essential_background_publications_ht...)

6. *Ibid*

7. *Ibid*

8. Climate Change Timeline: Climate Change Wales (http://www.climatechangewales.org.uk/ public/?id=121)

9. *ibid*

10. Unravelling the climate change story|GRID-Arendal-Publications-V (hrrp://www.grida.no/publications/ vg/climate2/page/2648.aspx)
There is general permission to use this mater vide http://www.grida.no/general/2832.aspx.

At the beginning of the 20th century annual global oil output was 150 million barrels of oil. Now that amount is extracted In just two days.(www.global-greenhouse-warming.com/what is global warming)

Box 5.

Chapter 6

GREENHOUSE GASES

The basic scientific conclusions on climate change are very robust and for good reason. The greenhouse effect is simple science: greenhouse gases trap heat, and humans are emitting ever more greenhouse gases. Nicholas Stern

In the preceding chapter we have seen how a blanket of gases causes warming effect. We have also seen that by drawing analogy from a greenhouse, the phenomenon is called the *greenhouse effect*. As a corollary to the same, the gases that cause warming effect have been named *greenhouse gases*. We have also seen which these gases are. We shall now see their brief descriptions, increasing concentration levels, sources etc. The current concentration of greenhouse gases in the atmosphere is the net result of its past emissions and removals from the atmosphere.

To begin with definition, the IPCC, in its of glossary of terms,[1] defines greenhouse gases as: "Greenhouse gases are those gaseous constituents of the *atmosphere*, both natural and *anthropogenic*, that absorb and emit radiation at specific wavelengths within the spectrum of *infrared radiation* emitted by the earth's surface, the atmosphere, and clouds. This property causes the *greenhouse effect*. Water vapor (H_2O), *carbon dioxide* (CO_2), *nitrous oxide* (N_2O), *methane* (CH_4), and *ozone* (O_3) are the primary greenhouse gases in the Earth's atmosphere. Moreover, there are a number of entirely human-made greenhouse gases in the atmosphere, such as the *halocarbons* and other chlorine and bromine containing substances, dealt with under the *Montreal Protocol*. Besides CO_2, N_2O, and CH_4, the *Kyoto Protocol* also deals with the greenhouse gases namely, *sulfur hexafluoride* (SF_6), *hydro-fluorocarbons* (HFCs) and *per-fluorocarbons* (PFCs)."

The UNFCCC, under the Glossary of CDM Terms [2] defines greenhouse gas as – "A greenhouse gas listed in Annex A to the Kyoto Protocol, unless otherwise specified in a particular methodology."

Annex A to the protocol gives the list as under-

Greenhouse gases- Carbon dioxide (CO_2), methane (CH_4), nitrous oxide (N_2O), hydroflourocarbons (HFCs), perfluorocarbons (PFCs), sulphur hexafluoride (SF_6)..

In the UNFCCC's definition water vapours and ozone are excluded; because water vapours and ozone being natural occurrences no action of their mitigation arises.

Atmospheric life and global warming potential of greenhouse gases

Long-lived greenhouse gases (LLGHGs), for example, carbon dioxide, methane and nitrous oxide are chemically stable and persist in the atmosphere over time scales of a decade or centuries or longer, so that their emission has a long-term influence on climate. Because these gases are long lived, they become well mixed throughout the atmosphere much faster than they are removed and their global concentrations can be accurately estimated from a few locations. Carbon dioxide does not have a specific lifetime because it is continuously cycled between the atmosphere, oceans and land biosphere and its net removal from the atmosphere involves a range of processes with different timescales.

Global-warming potential (GWP) is a relative measure of how much heat a greenhouse gas traps in the atmosphere. It compares the amount of heat trapped by a certain mass of the gas in question to the amount of heat trapped by a similar mass of carbon dioxide. A GWP is calculated over a specific time interval, commonly 20, 100 or 500 years. GWP is expressed as a factor of carbon dioxide (whose GWP is standardized to 1). For example, the 20 year GWP of methane is 86, which means that if the same mass of methane and carbon dioxide were introduced into the atmosphere, that methane will trap 86 times more heat than the carbon dioxide over the next 20 years.

Greenhouse gas	Chemical formula	Lifetime (years)	Global Warming Potential(Time Horizon) years(a, b, c) a	b	c
Carbon dioxide	CO2	variable	1	1	1
Methane	CH4	12+/- 3	56	21	6.5
Nitrous oxide	N2O	120	280	310	170

Source: Global Warming Potentials: UNFCCC[3] (https://unfccc.int/ghg_data/ items3285.php)

Rise in concentrations of carbon dioxide, methane and nitrous oxide.

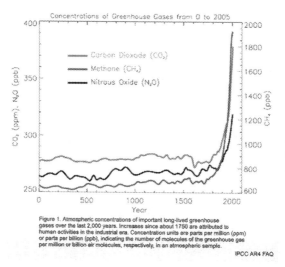

Fig. 6.1 IPCC FAQ 2.1 AR4,WGI[4]

The amount of CO_2 in the air increased from the level of 280 parts per million by volume (ppmv) at the pre-industrial to 389 ppmv at the end of 2010 (2014-395 ppmv). The amount of CO_2 varies throughout the year as the result of the annual cycles of photosynthesis and oxidation. Similarly, methane (CH_4) rose from a pre-industrial atmospheric concentration of around 700 parts per billion by volume (ppbv) to about 1813 ppbv by 2011 (2014-1893 ppbv). Nitrous oxide has risen from the pre-industrial level of 270 ppbv to 324 ppbv in 2011 (2014-326 ppbv). Of these, carbon dioxide is the single most important gas emitted by human activities that is responsible for over 60% of the enhanced greenhouse effect. Current annual emissions amount to over 23 billion metric tons of carbon dioxide[5].

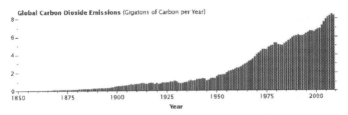

Fig. 6.2 (http://earthobservatory.nasa.gov/
Features/CarbonCycle/page4.php)

Emissions of carbon dioxide by humanity (primarily from the burning of fossil fuels, with a contribution from cement production) have been growing steadily since the onset of the industrial revolution. About half of these emissions are removed by the fast carbon cycle each year, the rest remain in the atmosphere. (Graph by Robert Simmon, using data from the <u>Carbon Dioxide Information Analysis Center</u> and <u>Global Carbon Project</u>.)

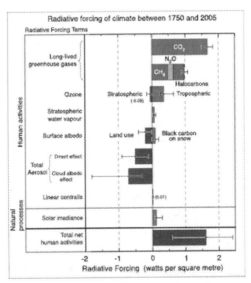

Fig. 6.3 (IPCC AR4, WGI, Chapter 2: <u>http://www.ipcc. ch</u> publications and data/ar4/wg1/faq-2.1 html)[6]

The contributions to radiative forcing from some of the factors influence by human activities(i.e. mostly of greenhouse gases) were shown by figure in the Fourth Assessment Report of the Working Group I, which epitomizes the influence cast by these factors between 1750-2005. The influence of a factor that can cause warming effect and consequently climate change, such as a greenhouse gas, is often evaluated in terms of its radiative forcing. Radiative forcing is a measure of how the energy balance of the Earth's system is influenced when factors that affect climate are altered. The figure is self-explanatory. It is seen that, among the greenhouse gases, carbon dioxide increases have caused the largest forcing over this period, followed by methane, nitrous oxide, halocarbons and tropospheric ozone[7].

Water Vapour:

"Water vapour is the most important greenhouse gas and the carbon dioxide is the second most important one[8]". It is also the most abundant one. Water vapours are formed through evaporation. Roughly 95% of evaporation comes from the oceans. It is a big contributor to the *natural greenhouse effect* and varies as per temperature. Cold air holds less water vapour. In contrast, as rise in temperature increases evaporation, hot air becomes humid. The contribution of water vapour to increase in global temperature is termed as 'positive feedback' as even a small increase in global temperature leads to a rise in global water vapour levels, further enhancing the greenhouse effect. According to NASA[9] carbon dioxide causes about 20 per cent of Earth's greenhouse effect; water vapour accounts for 50 per cent. It says:" Carbon dioxide molecules provide the initial greenhouse heating needed to maintain water vapor concentrations. When carbon dioxide concentrations drop, Earth cools, some water vapors fall out of the atmosphere, and the greenhouse warming by water vapor drops. Likewise, when carbon dioxide concentrations rise, air temperatures go up, and more water vapor evaporates into the atmosphere- which then amplifies greenhouse heating. So, while carbon dioxide contributes less to the overall greenhouse effect than water vapor, scientists have found *that carbon dioxide is the gas sets the temperature. Carbon dioxide controls the amount of water vapor in the atmosphere and thus the size of the greenhouse effect.*

Feedback role of water: The IPCC in its FAQ 1.3[10] explains: The amount of warming depends on various feedback mechanisms. For example, as the atmosphere warms due to rising levels of greenhouse gases, its concentration of water vapour increases, further intensifying the greenhouse effect. This, in turn causes more warming, which causes an additional increase in water vapour, in self-reinforcing cycle. The water vapour feedback may be strong enough to approximately double the increase in the greenhouse effect due to the added CO2 alone.

Carbon dioxide (CO_2)

A component of atmosphere, carbon dioxide is released through natural phenomena, such as respiration and volcano eruptions. It is a fundamental component of the earth's carbon cycle with considerable number of sources both natural and man- made. It is also a by-product of burning fossil fuels and biomass, as well as land-use changes and industrial processes. It is the principal *anthropogenic greenhouse gas* that affects the Earth's *radiative balance*. It is the reference gas against which other greenhouse gases are measured and therefore has a *Global Warming Potential* of 1. Although respiration is a large source of carbon dioxide it is currently smaller than the amount of CO_2 that is removed from the atmosphere annually, by photosynthesis. Its concentration in the atmosphere is as low as 0.039% (about 390 molecules per million)

Carbon dioxide produced by human activity enters the natural carbon cycle. Many billion tonnes of carbon are exchanged naturally each year between the atmosphere, the oceans, and land vegetation. The exchanges in this massive and complex natural system are precisely balanced; carbon dioxide levels appear to have varied by less than 10% during the 10,000 years before industrialization. Since 1800, however levels have risen by over 30%. Even with half of humanity's carbon dioxide emissions being absorbed by the oceans and land vegetation, atmospheric levels continue to rise by over 10% every 20 years[11]. Carbon dioxide from the burning of fossil fuels is the largest single source of greenhouse emissions from human activities. The supply and use of fossil fuels accounts for about 80 per cent of mankind's carbon dioxide.

According to the figures given in the context of the UN-REDD Programme (a forest development and conservation programme) "deforestation and forest degradation through agriculture expansion, conversion to pastureland, infrastructure development, destructive logging, fires etc. account for nearly 20% of global greenhouse gas missions[12]" The IPCC in its Fourth Assessment Report had estimated the percentage of deforestation in the total greenhouse gas emissions as 17. *Volcanoes* are relatively minor on global scale and account for less than 1% of yearly human geared CO_2 emissions.

Since the beginning of the Industrial Revolution, when people first started burning fossil fuels, carbon dioxide concentrations in the atmosphere have risen from about 280 parts per million to 387 parts per million, a 39 percent increase. This means that for every million molecules in the atmosphere, 387 of them are now carbon dioxide— the highest concentration in two million years. Methane concentrations have risen from 715 parts per billion in 1750 to 1,774 parts per billion in 2005, the highest concentration in at least 650,000 years.[13]

Carbon dioxide concentration measurement and monitoring

The build up of carbon dioxide in the atmosphere is measured by Keeling Curve. Charles Keeling was an American scientist, whose recording of carbon dioxide at Mauna Loa Laboratory (1958-1961) alerted the world to the possibility of anthropogenic contribution to the 'greenhouse effect' and global warming. Mauna Loa in Hawaii is above 3,000 m above sea level. Dr. Keeling started collecting carbon dioxide samples at the base in 1958. In 1961 Dr. Keeling produced data showing that carbon dioxide levels were rising steadily in what came to be known as Keeling Curve. The global concentration of carbon is closely monitored, analyzed and circulated. For this purpose the Carbon Dioxide Information Analysis Center (CDIAC) is the primary climate-change data and information analysis center of the U.S. Department of Energy (DOE). CDIAC is located at DOE's Oak Ridge National Laboratory (ORNL) and includes the World Data Center for Atmospheric Trace Gases[14]

According to the report of the Global Carbon Project of the CDIAC for 2013, global emissions of carbon dioxide from the combustion of fossil fuels were 36 billion tonnes for the year 2013.The estimates for 2014 are 40 billion tonnes. GCP provides an annual report of carbon dioxide emissions, land and ocean sinks and accumulation in the atmosphere, incorporating data from multiple research institutes from around the world[15].

Methane (CH_4)

Methane exists in much smaller quantities in the atmosphere than carbon dioxide. Its abundance is measured in parts per billion (ppbv). Its sources include landfills, natural gas flaring, cows, buffaloes, rice cultivation and coal mining. Even though its concentration is lower than carbon dioxide, its warming effect is *25* times as much as CO_2 as its Global Warming Potential is 25. However its effective atmospheric lifetime is of only 12 years. Thus, due to its much less abundance and its short effective atmospheric life, its contribution to global warming is less than that of carbon dioxide. Methane accounts for 20% of the enhanced greenhouse effect. It is estimated that about two thirds of global methane comes from man-made sources such as burning of fossil fuels, incidental release during drilling for natural gas or from cattle ranching. Since the Industrial Revolution the level of methane in the atmosphere has increased by about two and half times (259%) i.e. from the pre-industrial level of 700 ppb to 1812 ppb in 2011. Recently its rise is reported to be more and the process of its removal is difficult to predict[16]

Nitrous oxide (N_2O)

Nitrous oxide is the third most contributor to the radiative forcing by LLGHGs, as its contribution is 6%. to radiative forcing. Among greenhouse gases, its proportion is very small (less than one thousandth of carbon dioxide). However, it is 200 to 300 times more effective in trapping heat than carbon dioxide. Nitrous oxide *contributes 6% to radiative forcing by LLHGS*. Its Global Warming Potential is 298. It has long atmosphere lifetime as it remains in the atmosphere up to 150 years. Nitrous oxide is emitted into the atmosphere from both natural (about 60%) and anthropogenic sources (approximately 40%), including oceans, soil, biomass burning, fertilizer use and various industrial processes. The average global N_2O mole fraction in 2011 reached 324 ppb which is 120% of the pre-industrial level of 270 ppb. Nitrous oxide also enters the atmosphere from the oceans. Burning fossil fuels and wood is one source of the increase of nitrous oxide in the atmosphere[17]. A major contributor of the increase of nitrous oxide in the atmosphere is the use of nitrogenous fertilizers. Sewage treatment plants are also a major source of this gas. According to the information contained in Critical Reviews in Plant Sciences 22(5) – 453,[18] about 100 million tones of nitrogen is used every year for agriculture production.

Ozone: The atmospheric distribution of ozone and its role in the Earth's energy budget is unique. Ozone in the lower part of the atmosphere, the troposphere and lower stratosphere, acts as a greenhouse gas. Higher up in the stratosphere there is a natural layer of high ozone concentration, which absorbs solar ultra-violet radiation. In this way this so-called ozone layer plays an essential role in the stratosphere's radiative balance, at the same time filtering out this potentially damaging form of radiation[19].

Other greenhouse gases: These are Hydroflourocarbons, (HFCs), Perfluorocarbons(PFCs) Sulphur hexafluoride(SF6) etc. These are industrial gases. They are more potent than other greenhouse gases and have a longer atmospheric life. But their abundance is very small. Chlorofluorocarbons have been banned by Montreal Protocol in 1985.

Emissions of greenhouse gases from agriculture and livestock

Rice cultivation

According to the UNFCCC[20], "Wetland or paddy rice farming produces roughly one-fifth to one quarter of global methane emissions from human activities. Accounting for 90 per cent of all rice production, wetland rice is grown in fields that are flooded or irrigated for much of the growing season. Bacteria and other micro-organisms in the soil of the flooded rice paddy decompose organic matter and produce methane"

Rice cultivation is also a sequester of carbon dioxide

The above cited study of FAO further says: "In 2004, for example the global paddy rice output was 607.3 million tones at 14% moisture content. At the grain / straw ratio of 0.9 for most currently planted rice varieties, the global rice straw output in 2004 was about 676 million tones at 14% moisture content. This means that in 2004, rice sequestered about 1.74 billion tonnes of CO_2 from the atmosphere to produce 1.16 billion tonnes of bio-mass at 0% moisture content."

Livestock as a major contributor of greenhouse gases

As stated in the UNFCCC – Climate Change Information Sheet 22[21] the second most important "greenhouse gas after carbon dioxide, methane is produced by cattle, dairy cows, buffalo, goats, sheep, camels, pigs and horses.

Most live-stock related methane is produced by enteric fermentation of food by bacteria and other microbes in the animal's digestive tracts. Another source is the decomposition of animal manure. Livestock accounts for 30% of the methane emissions from human activities.

The Food and Agriculture Organization in its news release of 29 November, 2006[22] says as under-

"Which causes more greenhouse gas emissions, rearing cattle or driving cars?"

The news says – "The livestock sector generates more greenhouse gas emissions as measured in CO_2 equivalent (i.e. quantity of methane is converted into CO_2 based on its global warming potential).

The news further says that "with increased prosperity, people are consuming more meat and dairy products every year. Global meat production is projected to more than double from 229 millions in 1999 / 2001 to 465 million tones in 2050, while milk output is set to climb from 580 to 1043 million tones."

"The fastest growing global livestock sector provides livelihoods to 1.3 billion people.

When emissions from land use and land use change are included, the livestock sector accounts for 9% of CO_2 deriving from human related activities, but produces a much larger share of even more harmful greenhouse gases. It generates 65% of human related nitrous oxide, which has 296 times the Global Warming Potential (GWP) of CO_2. Most of this comes from manure."

"And it accounts for respectively 37% of all human induced methane (23 times as warming as CO_2), which is largely produced by the digestive system of ruminants, and 64% of ammonia, which contributes to acid rain. Livestock now use 30% of the earth's entire land surface, mostly permanent pasture but also including 33% of the global arable land used to producing feed for livestock, the report notes. As forests are cleared to create new pastures, it is a major driver of deforestation, especially in Latin America here, for example, some 70% of former forests in the Amazon have been turned over to grazing."

Land and water

"At the same time herds cause wide-scale land degradation, with about 20% of pastures considered as degraded through overgrazing, compaction and erosion. This figure is even higher in the dry lands where inappropriate policies and inadequate livestock management contribute to advancing desertification.

UNFCCC Graphic [23]

Share of global greenhouse gas emissions by major sectors

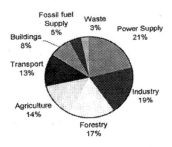

Fig. 6.5

Emitter Nations

Present concentrations of greenhouse gases are the result of emissions that have been taking place from the industrial revolution (1850). The valuable data of historical emissions comes from the publication of the World Resources Institute[24].

Cumulative Co$_2$ Emissions

1850 – 2002

Country	% of world	Rank
United States	29.3	1
EU – 25	26.5	2
Russia	8.1	3
China	7.6	4
Germany	7.3	5
United Kingdom	6.3	6

Japan	4.1	7
France	2.9	8
India	2.2	9
Ukraine	2.2	10
Canada	2.1	11
Poland	2.1	12
Italy	1.6	13
South Africa	1.2	14
Australia	1.1	15
Mexico	1.0	16
Spain	0.9	20
Brazil	0.8	22
South Korea	0.8	23
Iran	0.6	24
Indonesia	0.5	27
Saudi Arabia	0.5	28
Argentina	0.5	29
Turkey	0.4	31
Pakistan	0.2	48

Source: World Resources Institute-Climate Analysis Indicators Tool

Country-wise per capita carbon dioxide emissions

Historically these are the U.S.A. and the European countries who have contributed most to the pent up of carbon dioxide in the global atmosphere. Presently China and India appear among the big emitter countries in terms of total amount of emissions. However, what effectively matters is the per capita consumption.

EDGAR (data base created by European Commission and Netherland Assessment Agency) released 2012 estimates[25]. The following table lists the 2012 estimate of annual CO_2 emissions estimates (in thousands of CO_2 tonnes) from these estimates, along with a list of emissions per capita (in tonnes of CO_2 per year) from the same source.

Country	CO2 emissions	Emissions per capita
World	34,500,000	4.9
China	9,860,000	7.1
United States	5,190,000	16.4
India	1,970,000	1.6
Russia	1,770,000	12.4
Japan	1,320,10.4	10.4
International transport	1,060,000	-
Germany	810,000	9.7
South Korea	640,000	13.0
Canada	560,000	16.0
United Kingdom	490,000	7.7
Mexico	490,000	4.0
Indonesia	490,000	2.0
Saudi Arabia	460,000	16.2
Brazil	460,000	2.3
Australia	430,000	18.8
Iran	410,000	5.3
Italy	390,000	6.3

France	370,000	6.3
South Africa	330,000	6.3
Poland	320,000	8.4

In searching for a new enemy to unite us, we came up with the idea that pollution, the threat of global warming ..... would fit the bill .... All these dangers are caused by human interventions ...... and thus the "real enemy", then is the humanity ....

Club of Rome – Box 6 Box

Sources:

1. Glossary of terms-Annex B to the IPCC, TAR (www.ipcc.ch/pdf/glossary/tar)

2. UNFCCC Glossary of CDM terms (cdm.unfccc.int>Rules and references)

3. Global Warming Potentials: UNFCCC[3] (https://unfccc.int/ghg_data/ items3285.php)

4. IPCC, 2007: Climate Change 2007.: The Physical Science Basis:: Contribution of Working Group I to the Fourth Assessment Report of the Intergovernmental Panel on Climate Change [Solomon, S., D.Qin, M.Manning, Z.Chen, M.Marquis. K.B. Averyt, M.Tignor and H.L. Miller (eds.)]. Cambridge University Press, Cambridge, United Kingdom and New York, NY, USA. (FAQ 2.1 page 135)

5. Causes of Climate Change | WMO (http://www.wmo. int/pages/themes /climate/causes_of_climate_change. php)Informationofcurrentconcentrationofgreenhouse gases is from CDIAC (http://cdiac.ornl.gov/ current_ghg.html#)

6. IPCC, 2007 *op.cit* (FAQ 2.1 page 135)

7. IPCC, 2007 op.cit (FAQ 2.1 page 136)

8. IPCC,2007 op.cit (FAQ 1.3 page 115)

9. The Carbon Cycle: Feature Articles (http:// earthobservatory.nasa.gov/Features/CarbonCycle/ page.5 php)

10. IPCC, 2007, *op.cit* (FAQ 1.3 page 115)

11. UNFCCC Climate Change Information Sheet 3, (https:// unfccc.int/essential background publications.ht)

12. UN REDD Programme (http://www.un-redd.org/ aboutredd/tabid/102614/default.aspx)

13. Carbon Feature Articles ((http://earthobservatory. nasa.gov/Features/CarbonCycle/page4.php)

14. CDIAC (http://cdiac.esd.ornl.gov/GCP/ carbonbudget/2013/#)

15. *Ibid*

16. UNFCCC Climate Change Information Sheet 3, *op.cit*

17. WMO Bulletin November, 2012.

18. Critical Reviews in Plant Sciences 22 (5) 453- May 2012.(www.tandfonline.com)

19. The Climate System; an Overview (www.grida.no/ climate/ipcc-tar/pdf/tar.01)

20. UNFCCC Climate Change Information Sheet 22 (http://unfccc.int/essential_background/ background_publications_htmlp...)

21. *ibid*

22. FAO News release-29/11/2006.(www.FAO. org>Newsroom>News Stories 2006)

23. .UNFCCC Fact Sheet: The need for mitigation-November 2009.

24. WRI(2005)-Navigating the Numbers Greenhouse Data and International Climate Policy. (www.wri.org/ publication/navigating the numbers).

25. Wikipedia ((http://en.wikipedia.org/wiki/ List_of_countries_by_carbon_dioxide_emissions# List_of_countries_by_2012_emissions_estimates)

Chapter 7

CONSEQUENCES AND IMPACTS OF CLIMATE CHANGE

We learn from history that human life on the earth has always faced dangers and challenges. All along, mankind has suffered from calamities and survived. Throughout the history men have fought among themselves. Now a situation has come when mankind as a whole is facing a dire challenge of climate challenge. In the words of the IPCC ***"climate change will be unlike anything experienced by human civilization over the past 10,000 years."*** Climate change is not only an environmental problem but as well as a socio-economic problem, causing a wide range of consequences and impacts on the ecosystems and human systems. Now we have a body of scientists who tell us what exactly is going wrong, how it will affect us and what needs to be done. The intergovernmental Panel on Climate Change, has through its Assessment Reports coming after every 5-7 years has laid it bare for us, to act upon. Other bodies in the UN system, especially the UNFCCC and the WMO have analyzed the reports and examined the findings and collated them with the real situations, over the decades, and have categorized and summarized them into *information sheets*. Following are a few of the main contents from the information sheets of UNFCCC and WMO. Suggested action by the UNFCCC is shown in italics.

Warming-heat waves, droughts[1]

1. The earth has warmed. Eleven of the last twelve years rank among the warmest years in global surface temperatures since 1850.The rate of warming averaged over the last 100 years. More warming means increased risk of damage.
2. Heat waves have become more frequent over most land areas. One such heat wave in Europe caused about 35,000 deaths.
3. Intense tropical cyclone activity has increased in various regions of the world since 1970.

Water resources[2]

4. Adverse changes in the hydrological cycle. A warmer temperature causes more evaporation, makes the rain pattern less stable, producing more precipitation in the form of heavy rain bursts. This situation of more water, but not everywhere of rain leads to decline in quantity and quality of freshwater supplies in all regions of the world.

People exposed to increased water stress by 2020-

- 120 million to 1.2 billion in Asia.
- 75 to 250 million in Africa
- 12 to 81 million in Latin America[3].

5. Changing precipitation patterns are already affecting water supplies. Increasingly heavy rain and snow are falling on the mid and high latitudes of the Northern Hemisphere, while rains have decreased in the tropics and subtropics in both hemispheres. In large parts of Eastern Europe, western Russia, central Canada, and California, peak stream flows have shifted from spring to winter as more precipitation falls as rain rather than snow, therefore reaching the rivers more rapidly. Meanwhile, in Africa's large basins of the Niger, Lake Chad and Senegal, total available water has decreased by 40-60%.

6. Reduced water supplies would place additional stress on people, agriculture and the environment. Already, 1.7 billion people- a third of the world population-live in water stressed countries, a figure expected to rise to 5 billion by 2025. Climate change will exacerbate the stresses caused by pollution and by growing populations and economies. The most vulnerable regions are arid and semi-arid areas, some low-lying.

7. *Improved water resource management can help to reduce vulnerabilities. New supplies must be developed and existing supplies used more efficiently. Long-term strategies for supply and demand management could include: regulations and technologies for directly controlling land and water use, incentives and taxes for indirectly affecting behavior, the construction of new reservoirs and pipelines to boost supplies, improvements in water-management operations and institutions, and the encouragement of local or traditional solutions. Other adaptation measures can include protecting*

waterside vegetation, restoring river channels to their natural form, and reducing water pollution.

Biological Diversity and Ecosystem[4]

Photo 7. Pic Satyajit Shinde

Biological diversity-the source of enormous environmental, economic and cultural value-will be threatened by rapid climate change. The composition and geographic distribution of ecosystems will change as individual species respond to new conditions created by climate change. Scientists have observed climate-induced changes in at least 420 physical processes and biological species or communities.

8. Melting of glaciers and declining snow covers have contributed to a rise of sea level that has worsened coastal flooding and erosion, and has created a risk of displacement of people living near the coasts.

9. The oceans are experiencing higher temperatures, which have affected the marine life. Acidification of the oceans, as a result of rise in carbon dioxide concentrations, has made the oceans more acidic, which is affecting the ability of corals, marine snails and other species to form their shells.

10. Many ecosystems are already responding to higher temperatures and are moving towards poles and mountainsides. 20-30 % of species are likely to be at risk of extinction, if increases in warming further exceed exceed.

11. Mountain regions are already under considerable stress from human activities. The projected declines in mountain glaciers, permafrost, and snow cover will further affect soil stability and hydrological systems (most major river systems start in the mountains). As species and ecosystems are forced to migrate uphill, those limited to mountain tops may have nowhere to go and become extinct; observations show that some plant species are moving in the European Alps by one to four meters per decade and that some mountaintop species have already disappeared. Agriculture, tourism hydropower, logging and other economic activities will also be affected. The food and fuel resources of indigenous populations in many developing countries may be disrupted.

12. The cryosphere will continue to shrink. Representing nearly 80% of all freshwater, the cryosphere encompasses all of the earth's snow, ice and permafrost. Permafrost is thawing worldwide- even around Siberia's Lake Baikal, the coldest place in the Northern Hemisphere-destabilizing infrastructure and releasing additional carbon and methane into the atmosphere. Mountain glaciers are declining: almost two thirds of Himalayan glaciers have retreated in the past decade, and Andean glaciers have retreated dramatically or disappeared.

13. *Human actions can help natural ecosystems adapt to climate change. Creating natural migration corridors and assisting particular species to migrate could benefit forest ecosystems. Reforestation and the "integrated management" of fires, pests, and diseases can also contribute. Rangelands could be*

supported through the active selection of plant species, controls on animal stocking, and new grazing strategies. Wetlands can be restored and even created. Desertified lands may adapt better if drought-tolerant species and better soil conservation practices are encouraged.

Sea-level, oceans, and coastal areas[5]

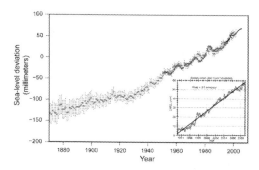

Fig. 7 (Credit: www.ncdc.noaa.gov- ww.ncdc.noaa.go
v%25252Findicators%25252F&source=iu&pf)

The global average sea-level has risen by 10-20 cm over the past 100 years. The rate of increase has been 1-2 mm per year- 10 times faster than the rate observed for the previous 3,000 years. It is likely that much of this rise is related to an increase of 0.6+/-0.2⁰C in the lower atmosphere's global temperature since 1860. Related effects now being detected include warming sea-surface temperatures, melting ice, greater evaporation, and changes in the marine food web.

14. Models project that sea levels will rise another 9 to 88 cm by the year 2100. This will occur due to the thermal expansion of warming ocean and influx of freshwater from melting glaciers and ice.

15. Flooding and coastal erosion would worsen. Salt water intrusion will reduce the quality and quantity of freshwater supplies. Higher sea levels could also cause extreme events such as high tides, storm surges, and seismic sea waves (tsunami) to reap more destruction. Developing countries with weaker economies, low-lying and island countries and even the low-lying coastal zones of the developed countries could also be severely affected. Already, over the past 100 years, 70% of sandy shorelines have been retreating.

16. Various natural forces will influence the impact that higher sea levels will have. Coastal areas are dynamic systems. Sedimentation, physical or biotic defenses (such as coral reefs), and other local conditions will interact with rising sea-water. The survival of salt marshes and mangrove forests will depend in part on whether the rate of sedimentation is greater than or less than the rate of local sea-level rise. Sedimentation is more likely to exceed sea level rise in sediment rich regions such as Australia, where strong tidal currents redistribute sediments.

17. Sea-level rise could damage key economic sectors. A great deal of food is produced in coastal areas, making fisheries, aquaculture, and agriculture particularly vulnerable. The expected sea -level rise would inundate much of the world's lowlands, damaging coastal cropland and displacing millions of people from coastal and small-island communities.

18. Ocean ecosystems may also be affected. In addition to higher sea levels, climate change will reduce ice-cover; decreases of up to 14% have been measured in the Arctic during the past two decades, and a decline

of 25% has been recorded in the Antarctic from the mid-1950s to early 1970s. Climate change will also alter ocean circulation patterns, the vertical mixing of waters, and wave patterns. These changes can be expected to affect biological productivity, the availability of nutrients, and the ecological structure and functions of marine ecosystems.

19. *Many policy options are available for adapting to sea-level rise. Sensitive environmental, economic, social and cultural values are at stake, and trade-offs may be unavoidable. Possible response strategies include protection (dikes, dune restoration, wetland creation), accommodation (new building codes, protection of threatened ecosystems), and planned retreat (regulations against new coastal development). Some countries, including Australia, China, Japan, the Netherlands, the UK and the US, have already designated withdrawal corridors where buildings will be removed to allow precious wetlands to move inland. Other specific responses are dredging ports, strengthening fisheries management, and improving design standards for offshore structures.*

Climate disasters and extreme events[6]

Natural variability of climate often leads to climate extremes. Growing human vulnerability is transforming more and more extreme events into climatic disasters as growing number of people are forced to live in exposed and marginal areas. More hot weather will cause more deaths and illnesses among the elderly and urban poor. Together with increased summer drying, it will lead to greater heat stress for livestock and wildlife, more damage to crops more forest fires and more pressure on water supplies.

20. The intensity of tropical cyclones is likely to worsen over some areas. The risks include direct threats to human life, epidemics and other health risks, damage to infrastructure and buildings, coastal erosion, and destruction of ecosystems such as coral reefs and mangroves.

21. *While extreme events are inherently abrupt and random, the risks they pose can be reduced. Improved preparedness planning is urgently needed in many parts of the world, with or without climate change. Better information, stronger institutions, and new technologies can minimize human material losses. For example, new buildings can be designed and located in ways that minimize damage from floods and tropical cyclones, while sophisticated irrigation techniques can protect farmers and their crops from droughts.*

Infrastructure, industry and human settlements[7]

22. Climate change will affect human settlements. Settlements that depend heavily on commercial fishing, subsistence agriculture and other natural resources are particularly vulnerable. Also at risk are low-lying areas and deltas, large coastal cities, squatter camps located in flood plains and on steep hillsides, settlements in forested areas where seasonal wildfires may increase, and settlements stressed by population growth, poverty and environmental degradation, in all cases, the poorest people will be the most affected. Infrastructure will become vulnerable to flooding and landslides.

23. Warming, dryness and flooding could undermine water supplies. Settlements in regions that are already water deficient- including much of North Africa, the Middle East, Southwest Asia, portions of western North America and some Pacific islands- can be expected to face still higher demands for water, as the climate warms.

24. Agriculture and fisheries are sensitive to climate change. In some cases agricultural yields may be reduced by up to several tens of percent as a result of hotter weather, greater evaporation, and lower precipitation, particularly in mid-continental growing regions. However, other regions may benefit and could experience higher yields. Fisheries will be affected because changes in ocean conditions caused by warming can substantially impact the locations and types of target species.

25. Sea-level rise will affect coastal infrastructure and resource-based industries. Many coastlines are highly developed and contain human settlements, industry, ports and other infrastructure. Many of the most vulnerable regions include some small island nations, low-lying deltas in developing countries and densely populated coasts that currently lack extensive sea and coastal defense systems. Several industries such as tourism and recreation- the principal earners for many island economies- are particularly dependent on coastal resources.

26. Energy demand is sensitive to climate change. Energy supplies will be vulnerable to changes resulting from global warming. For example, increased water deficits, less winter snowfall to fill

summer streams, and more demand for freshwater supplies would affect hydropower production.

27. Infrastructure in permafrost regions is vulnerable to warming. Permafrost melting is a threat to infrastructure in these regions because it would increase landslides and reduce the stability of foundations for structures. Other impacts would include greater damage from freeze-thaw cycles In addition; melting permafrost is thought to be a source of methane and carbon dioxide emissions.

28. *Local capacity is critical to successful adaptation. The capacity of local communities to adapt tends to be strongly correlated with wealth, human capital and institutional strength. The most effective sustainable solutions are those that are strongly supported-and often developed-locally. The role of higher-level bodies is then to provide technical assistance and institutional support. A clear message for policy-makers is to always anticipate the likely future impacts of climate change when they take decisions regarding human settlements and make investments in infrastructure.*

Health[8]

29. Climate change is expected to have wide-ranging consequences for human health. Public health depends on sufficient food, safe drinking water, secure shelter, good social conditions, and a suitable environmental and social setting for controlling infectious diseases. All of these factors can be affected by climate change.

30. Heat waves are linked to cardiovascular, respiratory, and other diseases. Illness and

deaths from these causes could be expected to increase, especially for the elderly and the urban poor. While the biggest rise in heat stress is expected in mid-and high latitude cities, milder winters in temperate climates would probably reduce cold-related deaths in some countries. A greater frequency of warm hot weather, thermal inversions (a meteorological phenomenon that can delay the dispersal of pollutants), and wildfires may also worsen air quality in many cities.

31. Any increase in the frequency or intensity of extreme weather events would pose a threat. Heat waves, flooding storms, and drought can cause deaths and injuries, famine, the displacement of populations, disease out- breaks, and psychological disorders. While scientists are uncertain just how climate change will affect storm frequency, they do project that certain regions will experience increased flooding or drought. In addition, coastal flooding is expected to worsen due to sea-level rise unless sea defenses are upgraded.

32. Higher temperatures may alter the geographical distribution of species that transmit disease. In a warmer world, mosquitoes, ticks and rodents could expand their range to higher latitudes and higher altitudes. Climate change impact models suggest that the largest changes in the potential for malaria transmission will occur at the fringes-in terms of both latitude and altitude-of the current malaria risk areas; generally, people in these border areas will not have developed immunity to the disease. The seasonal transmission and distribution of many other diseases that are transmitted by mosquitoes (dengue, yellow fever)

and by ticks (Lyme disease, Hantavirus pulmonary syndrome, and tick-borne encephalitis) may also increase by climate change. In addition, climate-induced changes in the formation and persistence of pollens, spores and certain pollutants could promote more asthma, allergic disorders, and cardio-respiratory diseases.

33. Warmer seas could also influence the spread of diseases. Studies using remote sensing have shown a correlation between cholera cases and sea surface temperature in the Bay of Bengal. There is also evidence of an association between El Nino (which warms the waters of the south-western pacific) and epidemics of malaria and dengue. Enhanced production of aquatic pathogens and bio-toxins may jeopardize the safety of seafood. Warmer waters would also increase the occurrence of toxic algal blooms.

34. The poor communities who have fewer resources and already battling poverty like subsistence farmers, indigenous people and coastal population are most hit.

35. *People will have to adapt or intervene to minimize these enhanced health risks. Many effective measures are available. The most important, urgent, and cost-effective is to rebuild the public health infrastructure in countries where it has deteriorated in recent years. Many diseases and public health problems that can be exacerbated by climate change can be effectively prevented with adequate financial and human resources. Adaptation strategies can include infectious disease surveillance, sanitation programmes, disaster preparedness, improved water and pollution control, public education directed at*

personal behavior, training of researchers and health professionals, and the introduction of protective technologies such as housing improvements, air conditioning, water purification, and vaccination.

Agriculture and food security[9]

36. Global agriculture will face many challenges over the coming decades. Degrading soils and water resources will place enormous strains on achieving food security for growing populations. These conditions may be worsened by climate change. While a global warming less than 2.5° C could have no significant effect on overall food production, a warming of more than 2.5° C could reduce global food supplies and contribute to higher food prices.

37. Some agricultural regions will be threatened by climate change, while others may benefit. The impact on crop yields will vary considerably. Added heat stress, shifting monsoons, and drier soils may reduce yields by as much as a third in the tropics and subtropics, where crops are already near their maximum heat tolerance. Mid-continental areas such as US grain belt, vast sections of mid-latitude Asia, sub-Saharan Africa and parts of Australia are all expected to experience drier and hotter conditions. Meanwhile, longer growing seasons and increased rains may boost yields in many temperate regions; records show that the season has already lengthened in the UK, Scandinavia. Europe and North America.

38. More carbon dioxide in the atmosphere could boost productivity. In principle, higher levels of CO_2 should stimulate photosynthesis in certain

plants. This is particularly true for so-called C3 plants because increased carbon dioxide tends to suppress their photo-respiration. C3 plants make up the majority of species globally, especially in cooler and water habitats, and include most crop species, such as wheat, rice, barley, cassava and potato. Experiments based on a 50% increase of current CO_2 concentrations have confirmed that "CO_2 fertilization" can increase mean yields of C3 crops by 15% under optimal conditions. C4 plants would also use water more efficiently, but the effects on yields would be smaller in the absence of water shortages. C4 plants include such tropical crops as maize, sugar cane, sorghum and millet, which are important for the food security of many developing countries, as well as pasture and forage grasses. These positive effects could be reduced by accompanying changes in temperature, precipitation, pests, and the availability of nutrients.

39. The most vulnerable people are the landless, poor, and isolated. Poor terms of trade, weak infrastructure, lack of access to technology and information, and armed conflict will make it more difficult for these people to cope with the agricultural consequences of climate change. Many of the world's poorest areas, dependent on isolated agricultural systems in semi-arid and arid regions, face the greatest risk. Many at-risk populations live in sub-Saharan Africa, South, East and Southeast Asia; tropical areas of Latin America; and some Pacific island nations.

40. *Effective policies can help to improve food security. The negative effects of climate change can be limited*

by changes in crops and crop varieties, improved water-management and irrigation systems, adapted planting schedules and tillage practices, and better watershed management and land-use planning. In addition to addressing the physiological response of plants and animals, policies can seek to improve how production and distribution systems cope with fluctuations in yields.

References:

1. Climate change: harnessing knowledge towards a better future-WMO (http://www.wmo.int/pages/publications/Geneva_WMO_WMD_25_March08.p)

2. UNFCCC Climate Change Information Sheet 13 (http://unfccc.int/essential_background_publications_ht..)

3. Climate change: harnessing ...*op.cit*

4. UNFCCC Climate Change Information Sheet 12 (http://unfccc.int/essential_background_publications_ht..)

5. UNFCCC Climate Change Information Sheet 11 (http://unfccc.int/essential_background_publications_ht..)

6. UNFCCC Climate Change Information Sheet 16 (http://unfccc.int/essential_background_publications_ht..)

7. UNFCCC Climate Change Information Sheet 15(http://unfccc.int/essential_background_publications_ht..)

8. UNFCCC Climate Change Information Sheet 14 (http://unfccc.int/essential_background_publications_ht..)

9. UNFCCC Climate Change Information Sheet 10 (http://unfccc.int/essential_background_publications_ht..)

Chapter 8

FIFTH ASSESSMENT REPORT OF IPCC

Report of Working Group I –The Physical Science Basis

The Working Group I contribution to the IPCC's Fifth Assessment Report (AR5) considers new evidence of climate change based on many independent scientific analyses from observations of the climate system, paleoclimate archives, theoretical studies of climate processes and simulations using climate models. It builds upon the Working Group I contribution to the IPCC's Fourth Assessment Report (AR4), and incorporates subsequent new findings of research. As a component of the fifth assessment cycle, the IPCC Special Report on Managing the Risks of Extreme Events and Disasters to Advance Climate Change Adaptation (SREX) is an important basis for information on changing weather and climate extremes.

The Summary for Policy Makers (SPM) of the Fifth Assessment Report (AR5) of the Working Group I- Physical Science Basis, was made public on 27th September, 2013. These findings, conclusions supersede the relevant contents of the Fourth Assessment Report 2007- (AR4), although some of the present conclusions are in the nature of re-iterations of the conclusions of AR4.

The report is of about 1500 pages. The IPCC while releasing this report has put the Summary for Policy Makers (SPM) for public information. (Citation, in the manner required by IPCC given in References below). A very brief points like summary of some of the key findings, conclusions and projections, as were reported in the press, from the SPM, are mentioned here.

B. Observed Changes in the Climate System

1. Warming of the climate system is unequivocal, and since the 1950s, many of the observed changes are unprecedented over decades to millennia. The atmosphere and ocean have warmed, the amounts of snow and ice have diminished, sea level has risen, and the concentrations of greenhouse gases have increased

B.1 Atmosphere

Each of the last three decades has been successively warmer at the Earth's surface than any preceding decade since 1850. In the Northern Hemisphere, 1983–2012 was *likely* the warmest 30-year period of the last 1400 years.

The globally averaged combined land and ocean surface temperature data as calculated by a linear trend, show a warming of **0.85 [0.65 to 1.06] °C, over the period 1880–2012,** when multiple independently produced datasets exist. The total increase between the average of the 1850–1900 period and the 2003–2012 period is 0.78 [0.72 to 0.85] °C, based on the single longest dataset available. Changes in many extreme weather and climate events have been observed since about 1950. It is *very likely* that the number of cold days and nights has decreased and the number of warm days and nights has increased on the global scale.

B.2 Ocean

Ocean warming dominates the increase in energy stored in the climate system, accounting for more than 90% of the energy accumulated between 1971 and 2010 (*high confidence*). It is *virtually certain* that the upper ocean (0–700 m) warmed from 1971 to 2010 and it *likely* warmed between the 1870s and 1971. On a global scale, the ocean warming is largest near the surface, and the upper 75 m warmed by 0.11 [0.09 to 0.13] °C per decade over the period 1971–2010

B.3 Cryosphere

Over the last two decades, the Greenland and Antarctic ice sheets have been losing mass.

Glaciers have continued to shrink almost worldwide, and Arctic sea ice and Northern Hemisphere spring snow cover have continued to decrease in extent (*high confidence*)

B.4 Sea Level

The rate of sea level rise since the mid-19th century has been larger than the mean rate during the previous two millennia (*high confidence*). Over the period **1901–2010, global mean sea level rose by 0.19 [0.17 to 0.21] m.**

B.5 Carbon and Other Biogeochemical Cycles

The atmospheric concentrations of carbon dioxide (CO_2), methane, and nitrous oxide have increased to levels unprecedented in at least the last 800,000 years. CO_2 concentrations have increased by 40% since pre-industrial times, primarily from fossil fuel emissions and secondarily from net land use change emissions. The ocean has absorbed about 30% of the emitted anthropogenic carbon dioxide, causing ocean acidification. Human influence on the climate system is clear. This is evident from the increasing greenhouse gas concentrations in the atmosphere, positive radiative forcing, observed warming, and understanding of the climate system.

C. Drivers of Climate Change

Total radiative forcing is positive, and has led to an uptake of energy by the climate system. The largest contribution to total radiative forcing is caused by the increase in the atmospheric concentration of CO_2 since 1750

D.1 Evaluation of Climate Models

Climate models have improved since the AR4. Models reproduce observed continental-scale surface temperature patterns and trends over many decades, including the more rapid warming since the mid-20th century and the cooling immediately following large volcanic eruptions (*veryhigh confidence)*

D.2 Quantification of Climate System Responses

Observational and model studies of temperature change, climate feedbacks and changes in the Earth's energy budget together provides confidence in the magnitude of global warming in response to past and future forcing. The net feedback from the combined effect of changes in water vapour, and differences between atmospheric and surface warming is *extremely likely* positive and therefore amplifies changes in climate. The net radiative feedback due to all cloud types combined is *likely* positive. Uncertainty in the sign and magnitude of the cloud feedback is due primarily to continuing uncertainty in the impact of warming on low clouds.

D.3 Detection and Attribution of Climate Change

Human influence has been detected in warming of the atmosphere and the ocean, in changes in the global water cycle, in reductions in snow and ice, in global mean sea level rise, and in changes in some climate extremes. This evidence for human influence has grown since AR4. It is *extremely likely* that human influence has been the dominant cause of the observed warming since the mid-20th century.

Based on the longest global surface temperature dataset available, the observed change between the average of the period 1850–1900 and of the AR5 reference period is 0.61 [0.55 to 0.67] °C. However, warming has occurred beyond the average of the AR5 reference period. Hence, this is not an estimate of historical warming to present. Continued emissions of greenhouse gases will cause further warming and changes in all components of the climate system. Limiting climate change will require substantial and sustained reductions of greenhouse gas emissions.

E.1 Atmosphere: Temperature

Global surface temperature change for the end of the 21st century is *likely* to exceed 1.5°C relative to 1850 to 1900 for all RCP* scenarios except RCP 2.6. It is *likely* to exceed 2°C for RCP 6.0 and RCP 8.5, and *more likely than not* to exceed 2°C for RCP 4.5. Warming will continue beyond 2100 under all RCP scenarios except RCP 2.6. Warming will continue to exhibit inter -annual-to-decadal variability and will not be regionally uniform.

The global mean surface temperature change for the period 2016–2035 relative to 1986–2005 will *likely* be in the range of 0.3°C to 0.7°C (*medium confidence*).

E.2 Atmosphere: Water Cycle

Changes in the global water cycle in response to the warming over the 21st century will not be uniform. The contrast in precipitation between wet and dry regions and between wet and dry seasons will increase, although there may be regional exceptions

E.4 Ocean

The global ocean will continue to warm during the 21st century. Heat will penetrate from the surface to the deep ocean and affect ocean circulation.

E.5 Cryosphere

It is *very likely* that the Arctic sea ice cover will continue to shrink and thin and that Northern Hemisphere spring snow cover will decrease during the 21st century as global mean surface temperature rises. Global glacier volume will further decrease

E.6 Sea Level

Global mean sea level will continue to rise during the 21st century. Under all RCP scenarios the rate of sea level rise will *very likely* exceed that observed during 1971–2010 due to increased ocean warming and increased loss of mass from glaciers and ice sheet.

E.7 Carbon and Other Biogeochemical Cycles

Climate change will affect carbon cycle processes in a way that will exacerbate the increase of CO_2 in the atmosphere (*high confidence*). Further uptake of carbon by the ocean will increase ocean acidification.

Ocean uptake of anthropogenic CO_2 will continue under all four RCPs through to 2100, with higher uptake for higher concentration pathways (*very high confidence*). The future evolution of the land carbon uptake is less certain.

E.8 Climate Stabilization, Climate Change Commitment and Irreversibility

Cumulative emissions of CO_2 largely determine global mean surface warming by the late 21st century and beyond. Most aspects of climate change will persist for many centuries even if emissions of CO_2 are stopped. This represents a substantial multi-century climate change commitment created by past, present and future emissions of CO_2.

(Sourced from IPCC WGIAR5-SPM_Approved27Sep2013.pdf)

*Representative Concentration Pathways (RCPs) are four <u>greenhouse gas</u> concentration (not emissions) trajectories adopted by the <u>IPCC</u> for its <u>fifth Assessment Report (AR5)</u>.

The pathways are used for climate modeling and research. They describe four possible climate futures, all of which are considered possible depending on how much greenhouse gases are emitted in the years to come. The four RCPs, RCP2.6, RCP4.5, RCP6, and RCP8.5, are named after a possible range of <u>radiative forcing</u> values in the year 2100 (+2.6, +4.5, +6.0, and +8.5 W/m^2, respectively).*(http://www.theguardian.com/ environment/climate-consensus-97-per-cent/2013/aug/30/ climate-change-rcp-handy-summary)*

Reference:

IPCC, 2013: Summary for Policymakers. In: Climate Change 2013: The Physical Science Basis. Contribution of Working Group I to the Fifth Assessment Report of the Intergovernmental Panel on Climate Change [Stocker, T.F., D. Qin, G.-K. Plattner, M. Tignor, S.K. Allen, J. Boschung, A. Nauels, Y. Xia, V. Bex and P.M. Midgley (eds.)]. Cambridge University Press, Cambridge, United Kingdom and New York, NY, USA. (IPCC WGI AR5_SPM_Final_pdf-

http://www.climatechange2013.org/images/report/ WG1AR5_SPM_FINAL.pdfIPCC)

2^0C Tipping point not far

The Fifth Assessment Report of the IPCC-Contribution of the Working Group I, the Physical Science Basis, released in September, 2013 stated that to limit the warming to a rise of 2 degrees C above pre-industrial levels, 1,000 gigatons (trillion tonnes) is the upper limit of carbon dioxide that can be emitted. However, by 2011, humans had already emitted 531 gigatons. Climate change experts believe that this limit could be crossed in the next 25 years. The report further said that the world has 2795 gigatons of carbon in the form of fossil-fuels and reserves. Burning just 10% of these would lead to crossing the tipping point.

Box 8

Chapter 9

IPCC FIFTH ASSESSMENT REPORT, 2014. CONTRIBUTION OF WORKING GROUP II- IMPACTS, ADAPTATION AND VULNERABILITIES- SUMMARY FOR POLICYMAKERS (SPM)

The above report was released on 31st March, 2013, in Yokohama. The report was contributed by 243 lead authors and 436 contributing authors from around the world. Twelve thousand peer reviewed scientific research studies are cited –double the amount of scientific literature cited in the previous IPCC report of 2007. Thus, it is a monumental work. The report is voluminous. The IPCC while releasing this report has put the Summary for Policy Makers (SPM) for public information.(Reference in the manner required by IPCC given in References below. A very brief points like summary of some of the key findings, conclusions and projections, as were reported in the press, from the SPM, are mentioned here.

ASSESSING AND MANAGING THE RISKS OF CLIMATE CHANGE

Human interference with the climate system is occurring, and climate change poses risks for human and natural systems. The assessment of impacts, adaptation, and vulnerability in the **Working Group II contribution to the IPCC's Fifth Assessment Report (WGII AR5)** evaluates how patterns of risks and potential benefits are shifting due to climate change. It considers how impacts and risks related to climate change can be reduced and managed through adaptation and mitigation. The report assesses needs, options, opportunities, constraints, resilience, limits, and other aspects associated with adaptation. Climate change involves complex interactions and changing likelihoods of diverse impacts. A focus on risk, which is new in this report, supports decision-making in the context of climate change, and complements other elements of the report. People and societies may perceive or rank risks and potential benefits differently, given diverse values and goals. Compared to past WGII reports, the WGII AR5 assesses a substantially larger knowledge base of relevant scientific, technical, and socioeconomic literature. Increased literature has facilitated comprehensive assessment across a broader set of topics and sectors, with expanded coverage of human systems, adaptation, and the ocean.

Observed impacts, vulnerability and exposure.

❖ In recent decades, changes in climate have caused impacts on natural and human systems on all continents and across the oceans.

- ❖ In many regions, changing precipitation or melting snow and ice are altering hydrological systems, affecting water resources in terms of quantity and quality.

- ❖ Many terrestrial, freshwater, and marine species have shifted their geographic ranges, seasonal activities, migration patterns abundances, and species interactions in response to ongoing climate change (*high confidence*).

- ❖ Based on many studies covering a wide of regions and crops, negative impacts of climate change on crop yields have been more common than positive impacts (*high confidence*).

- ❖ At present, world-wide burden of human ill-health from climate change is relatively small compared with effects of other stressors, and is not well quantified.

- ❖ Differences in vulnerability and exposure arise from non-climatic factors and from multi-dimensional inequalities often produced by uneven development processes (*very high confidence*).

- ❖ Impacts from recent climate change-related extremes, such as heat waves, droughts, floods, cyclones and wildfires reveal significant vulnerability and exposure of some ecosystems to current climate variability (*very high confidence*).

- ❖ Responding to climate-related risks involves decision making in a changing world, with continuing uncertainty about the severity and timing of climate change impacts and with limits to effectiveness of adaptation (*high confidence*).

- ❖ Adaptation and mitigation choices in the near-term will affect the risks of climate change throughout the 21st century (*high confidence*).

Key risks with high confidence, that span sectors and regions, each of which contributing to one or more *RFCs

> ➢ Risk of death, injury, ill-health, or disrupted livelihoods in low-lying coastal zones and small island developing states and other islands, due to storm surges, coastal flooding and sea-level rise.

> ➢ Risk of severe ill-health and disrupted livelihoods for large urban populations due to inland flooding in some regions.

> ➢ Systemic risks due to extreme weather events leading to breakdown of infrastructure networks and critical services such as electricity, water supply, and health and emergency services.

> ➢ Risk of mortality and morbidity during periods of extreme heat, particularly for vulnerable urban populations and those working outdoors in urban or rural areas (RFC 2-3).

> ➢ Risk of food insecurity and the breakdown of food systems linked to warming, drought, flooding, and precipitation variability and extremes, particularly for poorer populations in urban and rural settings. (RFC 2-4).

> ➢ Risk of loss of rural livelihoods and income due to insufficient access to drinking and irrigation water and reduced agricultural productivity, particularly for farmers and pastoralists with minimal capital in semi-arid regions.(RFC 2 and 3).

> ➢ Risk of loss of marine and coastal ecosystems, biodiversity, and ecosystem goods, functions, and services they provide for coastal livelihoods,

especially for fishing communities in the tropics and the Arctic.(RFC 1,2 and 4).

➢ Risk of loss of terrestrial land inland water ecosystems, biodiversity, and the ecosystem goods, functions, and service they provide for livelihoods (RFC1, 3 and 4).

➢ Increasing magnitudes of warming increase the likelihood of severe, pervasive and irreversible impacts.

➢ Climate related hazards exacerbate other stressors, often with negative outcomes for livelihoods, especially for people living in poverty (*high confidence*)

➢ Violent conflict increases vulnerability to climate change (*medium evidence and high agreement*)

Many key risks constitute particular challenges for the least developed countries and vulnerable communities, given their limited ability to cope.

Freshwater Resources

Climate change over the 21st century is projected to reduce renewable surface water and groundwater resources significantly in most dry sub-tropical regions (*robust evidence, high agreement*).

▪ A large fraction of both terrestrial and freshwater species faces increased extinction risk under projected climate change during and beyond the 21st century, especially as climate change interacts with other stressors, such as habitat modification, over-exploitation, pollution, and invasive species (*High confidence*).

Food security and food production systems

- For the major crops (wheat, rice, and maize) in tropical and temperate regions, climate change without adaptationis projected to negatively impact production for local temperature increases of 2^0 C or more above late 20th century levels, although individual locations may benefit (*medium confidence*).
- All aspects of food security are potentially affected by climate change, including food access, utilization, and price stability (*high confidence*).

Urban and rural areas

- Many global risks of climate change are concentrated in urban areas (*medium confidence*). Steps that build resilience and enable sustainable development can accelerate successful climate-change adaptation globally.
- Major future rural impacts are expected in the near term and beyond through impacts on water availability and supply, food security, and agricultural incomes, including shifts in production areas of food and non-food crops across the world (*high confidence*).

Key economic sectors and services

- ✓ For most economic sectors, the impact of drivers such as changes in population, age structure, income, technology, relative prices, lifestyle, regulation, and governance are projected to be large relative to the impacts of climate change (*medium evidence, high agreement*).
- ✓ Global economic impacts from climate change are difficult to estimate.

Human health

- • Until mid-century, projected climate change will impact human health mainly by exacerbating health problems that already exist (*very high confidence*). Throughout the 21st century, climate change is expected to lead to increases in ill-health in many regions and especially in developing countries with low income, as compared to a baseline without climate change (*high confidence*).

Human Security

- ❖ Climate change over the 21st century is projected to increase displacement of people (*medium evidence, high agreement*)
- ❖ Climate change can directly increase risks of violent conflicts in the form of civil war and inter-group violence by amplifying well-documented drivers of these conflicts such as poverty and economic shocks (*medium confidence*).

❖ The impacts of climate change on the critical infrastructure and territorial integrity of many states are expected to influence national security policies (*medium evidence, medium agreement*).

❖ Throughout the 21st century climate change impacts are projected to slow down economic growth, make poverty reduction more difficult, further erode food security and prolong existing and create new poverty traps, the latter particularly in urban areas and emerging hotspots of hunger (medium confidence).

Principles for effective adaptation

- Adaptation is place and context specific, with no single approach for reducing risks appropriate across all settings (*high confidence*).

- Adaptation planning and implementation can be enhanced through complementary actions across levels, from individuals to government (*high confidence*).

- A first step towards adaptation to future climate change is reducing vulnerability and exposure to present climate variability (*high confidence*). Strategies include actions with benefits for other objectives.

Reference:

IPCC, 2014: Summary for Policy Makers. In *Climate Change 2014:Impacts, Adaptation and Variability. Part A Global and Sectoral Aspects. Contribution of Working Group II to the Fifth Assessment Report of the Intergovernmental Panel on Climate Change:* [Field C.B. VR. Barros, D.J. Dukken, K.J. Mach, M.D. Mastrandrea, T.E. Billir, M. Chatterjee, K.L. Elbi, Y.O. Estrada, R.C. Genova, B. Girma, E.S. Kissel, A.N. Levy, S.MacCracken, P.R. Mastrandrea and L.L. White(eds.)] Cambridge University Press, Cambridge United Kingdom and New York, NY, USA pp1-32.- Online version put up for public. Summary for Policy Makers (http://ipcc-wg2.gov/AR5/images/uploads/WG2 AR5_SPM_FINAL_pdf)

- RFCs are different scenarios worked by the IPCC, depending on the courses of actions of mitigation and adaptation that would be taken, out of the alternatives and the expected resulting warming.

Chapter 10

IPCC FIFTH ASSESSMENT REPORT (2014)- WORKING GROUP III- MITIGATION OF CLIMATE CHANGE

The Working Group III Contribution to the IPCC's Fifth Assessment Report (AR5) assesses literature on the scientific, technological, environmental, economic and social aspects of mitigation of climate change. It builds upon the working Group III contribution to the IPCC Fourth Assessment Report (AR4), the Special Report on Renewable Energy Sources and Climate Change Mitigation (SRREN) and previous reports and incorporates subsequent new findings and research. The report also assesses mitigation options at different levels of governance and in different economic sectors, and the societal implications of different mitigation policies, but does not recommend any particular option for mitigation.

The WG III report was finalized in April, 2014.

A very brief point like summary of some of the key conclusions and recommendations, as were reported in the press, from the Summary of Policy Makers (SPM) is mentioned below;

Approaches to climate change mitigation

Mitigation is a human intervention to reduce the sources or enhance the sinks of greenhouse gases. Mitigation, together with adaptation to climate change, contributes to the objective expresses in Article 2 of the United Nations Framework Convention on Climate Change (UNFCCC):

The ultimate objective of this Convention and any related legal instruments that the Conference of the Parties may adopt is to achieve, in accordance with the relevant provisions of the Convention, stabilization of greenhouse gas concentrations in the atmosphere at a level that would prevent dangerous anthropogenic interference with the climate system. Such a level should be achieved within a time frame sufficient to allow ecosystems to adapt naturally to climate change, to ensure that food production is not threatened and to enable economic development to proceed in a sustainable manner.

Sustainable development and equity provide a basis for assessing climate policies and highlight the need for addressing the risks of climate change.

Effective mitigation will not be achieved if individual agents advance their own interests independently.

Many areas of climate policy-making involve value judgments and ethical considerations.

Climate policy intersects with other societal goals creating the possibility of co-benefits or adverse side-effects. These intersections, if well managed, can strengthen the basis for undertaking climate action.

Climate policy may be informed by a consideration of a diverse array of risks and uncertainties, some of which are difficult to measure, notably events that are of low probability but which would have a significant impact if they occur.

The design of climate policy is influenced by how individuals and organizations perceive risks and uncertainties and take them into account.

Trends in stocks and flows of greenhouse gases and their drivers

Total anthropogenic GHG emissions have continued to increase over 1970 to 2010 with larger absolute decadal increases toward the end of this period. (*high confidence*)

CO_2 emissions from fossil fuel combustion and industrial processes contributed about 78% of the total GHG emission increase from 1970 to 2010, with a similar percentage contribution for the period 2000-2010 (*high confidence*).

About half of cumulative anthropogenic CO_2 emissions between 1750 and 2010 have occurred in the last 40 years (*high confidence*).

Annual anthropogenic GHG emissions have increased by 10 GtCo2eq between 2000 and 2010, with this increase directly coming from energy supply (47%), industry (30%), transport (11%) and buildings (3%) sectors (*medium confidence*). Accounting for indirect emissions raises the contributions of the buildings and industry sectors. (*high confidence*).

Globally, economic and population growth continue to be the most important drivers of increases in CO2 emissions from fossil fuel combustion. The contribution of population growth between 2000 and 2010 remained roughly identical to the previous three decades, while the contribution of economic growth has risen sharply (*high confidence*).

Without additional efforts to reduce GHG emissions beyond those in place today, emissions growth is expected to persist driven by growth in global population and economic activities. Baseline scenarios, those without additional mitigation, result in global mean surface temperature increases in 2100 from 3.7 to 4.8°C compared to pre-industrial levels (median values; the range is 2.5° C to 7.8° C when including climate uncertainty (*high confidence*)

Mitigation pathways and measures in the context of sustainable development

Long-term mitigation pathways

There are multiple scenarios with a range of technological and behavioral options, with different characteristics and implications for sustainable development, that are consistent with different levels of mitigation.

Mitigation scenarios in which it is *likely* that the temperature change caused by anthropogenic GHG emissions can be kept to less than 2° C relative to pre-industrial levels are characterized by atmospheric concentrations in 2100 of about 450 ppm CO2eq (*high confidence*)

Scenarios reaching atmospheric concentration levels of about 450 ppm CO2eq by 2100 (consistent with a likely chance to keep temperature change below 2°C relative to pre-industrial levels) include substantial cuts in anthropogenic GHG emissions by mid-century through large –scale change in energy systems and potentially land use (*high confidence*).

Delaying mitigation efforts beyond those in place today through 2030 is estimated to substantially increase the difficulty of the transition to low longer-term emissions levels and narrow the range of options consistent with maintaining temperature change below 2°C relative to pre-industrial levels (*high confidence*).

Only a limited number of studies have explored scenarios that are more likely than not to bring temperature change back to below 1.5°C by 2100 relative to pre-industrial levels; these scenarios bring atmospheric concentrations to below 430 ppm CO2 eq by 2100 (*high confidence.*)

Mitigation scenarios reaching about 450 or 500 ppm CO2eq by 2100 show reduced costs for achieving air quality and energy security objectives, with significant co-benefits for human health, ecosystem impacts, and sufficiency of resources and resilience of the energy system; these scenarios did not quantify other co-benefits or adverse side-effects (*medium confidence.*)

Cross-sectoral mitigation pathways and measures

In baseline scenarios, GHG emissions are projected to grow in all sectors, except for net CO2 emissions in the

Agriculture, Forestry and Land Use (AFOLU sector) (*robust evidence, medium agreement*).

Mitigation scenarios reaching around 450 ppm CO2eq concentrations by 2100, show large-scale global changes in the energy supply sector (*robust evidence, high agreement*).

Efficiency enhancements and behavioural changes, in order to reduce energy demand compared to baseline scenarios without compromising development, form a key mitigation strategy in scenarios reaching atmospheric CO2 eq concentrations of about 450 or 500 ppm by 2100 (*robust evidence, high agreement.*)

Behaviour, lifestyle and culture have a considerable influence on energy use and associated emissions, with high mitigation potential in some sectors, in particular when complementing technological and structural change (medium evidence, medium agreement).

Energy Supply

In the baseline scenarios assessed in AR5, direct CO2 emissions from the energy supply sector are projected to almost double or even triple by 2050 compared to the level of 14.4 GtCo2/year in 2010, unless energy intensity improvements can be significantly accelerated beyond the historical development (*medium evidence, medium agreement*).

Decarbonizing (i.e. reducing the carbon intensity of) electricity generation is a key component of cost-effective mitigation strategies in achieving low-stabilization levels (430-530 ppm CO2eq); in most integrated modeling scenarios, decarbonization happens more rapidly in electricity generation than in the industry, building, and transport sectors (*medium evidence, medium agreement*).

Since AR4, many RE technologies have demonstrated substantial performance improvements and cost reductions, and a growing number of RE technologies have achieved a level of maturity to enable deployment at significant scale (*robust evidence, high agreement*).

Nuclear energy is a mature low-GHG emission source of base load power, but its share of global electricity generation has been declining (since 1993). Nuclear energy could make an increasing contribution to low-carbon energy supply, but a variety of barriers and risks exist (*robust evidence, high agreement*)

GHG emissions from energy supply can be reduced significantly by replacing current world average coal-fired power plants with modern, highly efficient natural gas combined-cycle power plants or combined heat and power plants, provided that natural gas is available and the fugitive emissions associated with extraction and supply are low or mitigated (*robust evidence, high agreement*)

Carbon dioxide capture and storage (CCS) technologies could reduce the lifecycle GHG emissions of fossil fuel power plants (*medium evidence, medium agreement*).

Energy end-use sectors

The **transport sector accounted for 27% of final energy use and 6.7 GtCo2** direct emissions in 2010, with baseline

CO2 emissions projected to approximately double by 2050 (*medium evidence, medium agreement*).

Technical and behavioural mitigation measures for all transport made, plus new infrastructure and urban redevelopment investments, could reduce final energy demand in 2050, by around 40% below the baseline, with the mitigation potential assessed to be higher than reported in the AR4 (robust evidence, high agreement).

The cost-effectiveness of different carbon reduction measures in the transport sector varies significantly with vehicle type and transport mode (*high confidence*).

Buildings

In 2010, the building sector accounted for around 32% final energy use and 8.8 GtCo2 emissions, including direct and indirect emissions, with energy demand projected to approximately double and Co2 emissions to increase by 50-150% by mid-century in baseline scenarios (*medium evidence, medium agreement*).

Recent advances in technologies, know-how and policies provide opportunities to stabilize or reduce global buildings sector energy use by mid-century (*robust evidence, high agreement*)

Lifestyle, culture and behavior significantly influence energy consumption in buildings (*limited evidence, high agreement*)

Industry

In 2010, the industry sector accounted for around 28% of final energy use, and 13 $GtCo_2$ emissions, including direct and indirect emissions as well as process emissions, with emissions projected to increase by 50-150% by 2050 in the baseline scenarios assessed in AR5, unless energy efficiency improvements are accelerated significantly (*medium evidence, medium agreement*).

The energy intensity of the industry sector could be directly reduced by about 25% compared to the current level through the wide-scale upgrading, replacement and deployment of best available technologies, particularly in countries where these are not in use and in non-energy intensive industries

CO_2 emissions dominate GHG emissions from industry, but there are also substantial mitigation opportunities for non-Co_2 gases (*robust evidence, high agreement*).

Important options for mitigation in waste management are waste reduction, followed by re-use, recycling and energy recovery (*robust evidence, high agreement*).

Agriculture, Forestry and Other Land Use (AFOLU)

The AFOLU sector accounts for about a quarter (~10-12$GtCo_2eq$/yr) of net anthropogenic GHG emissions mainly from deforestation, agricultural emissions from soil and nutrient management and livestock (*medium evidence, medium agreement*).

AFOLU plays a central role for food security and sustainable development. The most cost-effective mitigation options in forestry are afforestation, sustainable forest management and reducing deforestation, with large differences in their relative importance across regions. In agriculture, the most cost-effective mitigation options are cropland management, grazing land management, and restoration of organic soils (*medium evidence, high agreement*).

Bio-energy can play a critical role for mitigation, but there are issues to consider, such as the sustainability of practices and the efficiency of bio-energy systems (*limited evidence, medium agreement*)

Human Settlements, Infrastructure and Spatial Planning

Urbanization is a global trend and is associated with increases in income, and higher urban incomes are correlated with higher consumption of energy and emissions (*medium evidence, high agreement*).

The next two decades present a window of opportunity for mitigation in urban areas, as a large portion of the world's urban areas will be developed during this period (*limited evidence, high agreement*).

Sectoral and national policies

Substantial reductions in emissions would require large changes in investment patterns.

There is no widely agreed definition of what constitutes climate finance, but estimates of the financial flows associated with climate change mitigation and adaptation are available.

There has been a considerable increase in national and sub-national mitigation plans and strategies since AR4.

In some countries, tax –based policies specifically aimed at reducing GHG emissions – alongside technology and other policies – have helped to weaken the link between GHG emissions and GDP.

The reduction of subsidies for GHG-related activities in various sectors can achieve emission reductions, depending on the social and economic context.

In many countries, the private sector plays central roles in the processes that lead to emissions as well as to mitigation. Within appropriate enabling environments, the private sector, along with the public sector, can play an important role in financing mitigation (*medium evidence, high agreement*).

International cooperation

The United Nations Framework Convention on Climate Change (UNFCCC) is the main multi-lateral forum focused on addressing climate change, with nearly universal participation.

Existing and proposed international climate change cooperation arrangements vary in their focus and degree of centralization and coordination.

UNFCCC activities since 2007 have led to an increasing number of institutions and other arrangements for international climate change cooperation.

Policy linkages among regional, national and sub-national climate policies offer potential climate change mitigation and adaptation benefits (*medium evidence, medium agreement*).

Reference:

IPCC, 2014: Summary for Policymakers, In: Climate Change 2014, Mitigation of Climate Change. Contribution of Working Group III to the Fifth Assessment Report of the Intergovernmental Panel on Climate Change [Edenhofer, O., R. Pichs-Madruga, Y. Sokona, E. Farahani, S. Kadner, K. Seyboth, A. Adler, I. Baum, S. Brunner, P. Eickemeier, B. Kriemann, J. Savolainen, S. Schlömer, C. von Stechow, T. Zwickel and J.C. Minx (eds.)]. Cambridge University Press, Cambridge, United Kingdom and New York, NY, USA

Chapter 11

CLIMATIC EXTREME EVENTS

It is a fact that for the last two decades or so occurrence of extreme climatic events and natural disasters have increased in their frequency and their severity. According to World Meteorological Organization, "naturally occurring phenomena such as volcanic eruptions or El Nino and La nina events have always contributed to frame our climate, influenced temperatures or caused disasters like droughts and floods. But many of the extreme events of 2013 were consistent with what we would expect as a result of human-induced climate change. We saw heavier precipitation, more intense heat, and more damage from storm surges and coastal flooding as a result of sea level rise- as Typhoon Haiyan so tragically demonstrated in the Philippines. There is no standstill in global warming[1]."

Can individual Extreme Events be explained by Greenhouse Warming?

These were climatic extreme events, aberrations of climate etc. during the 1960s and 1970s that brought to attention that something is wrong with the climate that needs to be looked into. The scientific body of Intergovernmental Panel on Climate Change, set up in 1988, started its work to unravel the mystery, and since then the knowledge of humanity about the climate changes went through sea change. The climatic extreme events are on the rise is a fact. The moot point is whether, and to what extent the climatic extreme can be attributed to greenhouse warming. The IPCC has addressed the topic in the FAQ 9.1 in the Fourth Assessment Report of IPCC.

It has been established that climate change is a reality. It is also a fact that climate extreme events the world over are happening more frequently in recent decades. However, scientists are cautious in attributing any single climate extreme events to climate change. IPCC says[2] that-

1) Extreme events are caused by a combination of factors, and

2) a wide range of extreme events is a normal occurrence even in an unchanging climate. Nevertheless, analysis of the warming observed over the past century suggests that the likelihood of some extreme events, such as heat waves, has increased due to greenhouse warming, and that the likelihood of others, such as frost or extremely cold nights, has decreased. For example, a recent study estimates that human influence shave more than doubled the risk of a very hot European summer like that of 2003.

Referring to the hot European summer of 2003, it says that extreme events usually result from a combination of factors. Several factors contributed to the extremely hot European summer of 2003, including a persistent high pressure system that was associated with very clear skies and dry soil, which left more solar energy available to heat the land because the less energy was consumed to evaporate moisture from the soil. Similarly, the formation of a hurricane requires warm sea surface temperatures and specific atmospheric circulation conditions. Because some factors may be strongly affected by human activities, such as sea surface temperatures, but others may not, it is not simple to detect a human influence on a single, specific extreme event. In the case of the 2003 heat wave, a climate model was run including only historical changes in natural factors that affect the climate. Next, the model was run again including both human and natural factors, which produced a simulation of the evolution of the European climate that was much closer to that which had actually occurred. Based on these experiments, it was estimated that over the 20th century, human influences have more than doubled the risk of having a summer in Europe as hot as that of 2003, and that in the absence of human influences; the risk would probably have been one in many hundred years.

The value of such a probability-based approach - 'Does human influence change the likelihood of an event? is that it can be used to estimate the influence of external factors, such as increases in greenhouse gases, on the frequency of specific types of events, such as heat waves or frost. Nevertheless, careful statistical analyses are required, since the likelihood of individual extremes, such as a late-spring frost, could change due to changes in climate variability as well as changes in average climate conditions. Such analyses rely on climate-model based estimates of climate variability, and thus the climate models used should adequately represent that variability.

The same likelihood-based approach can be used to examine changes in frequency of heavy rainfall or floods. Climate models predict that human influences will cause an increase in many types of extreme events, including extreme rainfall. There is already evidence that, in recent decades, extreme rainfall has increased in some regions, leading to an increase in flooding.

References:

1. WMO Annual Climate Statement- Press Release No. 985 (http://www.wmo.;int/pages/mediacentre/press_relese/pr_985)

2. IPCC,2007: *The Physical Science Basis, Contribution of Working Group I to the Fourth Assessment Report of the Intergovernmental Panel on Climate Change* (Solomon, S.,D.Qin, M.Manning, Z.Chen, M.Marquis, K.B. Averyt, M.Tignor and H.L.Miller (eds.).Cambridge University Press, Cambridge, United Kingdom and New York, NY, USA.(FAQ 9.1 page 696)

Chapter 12

WORLD METEOROLOGICAL ORGANIZATION-PLAYING KEY ROLE IN CLIMATE MONITORING

The World Meteorological Organization (WMO) is an intergovernmental organization in the UN system, with a membership of 191 countries and territories. It is the successor to the International Meteorological Organization, which was founded in 1873. Established in 1950, WMO became a specialized agency of the United Nations in 1951. Since its establishment, WMO has played a key role in contributing to the safety and welfare of humanity. Under WMO's leadership and within the framework of WMO programmes, National Meteorological and Hydrological Services (NMHSs) of the respective countries contribute substantially to: (1) the protection of life and property against natural disasters; (2) safeguarding the environment; and (3) enhancing the economic and social well-being of all sectors of society in areas such as food security, water resources and transport. WMO promotes cooperation in the establishment of networks for making meteorological, climatological, hydrological and geophysical observations, as well as the exchange, processing and standardization of related data, and assists technology transfer, training and research.

WMO's Members are represented in the Organization through their Permanent Representative, usually the Director of the NMHS. WMO's institutional structure consists of -

(i)   The World Meteorological Congress, the supreme body of the Organization, which meets every 4 years,

(ii) the Executive Council, the executive body of the Organization, which is responsible to Congress,

(iii) eight technical commissions composed of experts designated by Members and responsible for studying meteorological and hydrological operational systems, applications and research, and

(iv) the WMO Secretariat, headed by the Secretary-General with headquarters in Geneva, Switzerland, where the office of all the WMO sponsored and co-sponsored programmes are also located.

WMO is the UN system's authoritative voice on the state and behavior of the Earth's atmosphere, its interaction with the oceans, the climate it produces and the resulting distribution of water resources.

WMO is the specialized agency of the United Nations responsible for:

1.   Coordination of climate and weather research.

2.   Development of standards and technical developments.

3. Operational cooperation and coordination among its Members States for observing, analysis, data exchange, and forecasting of weather, climate, water and related environmental conditions, and

4. Capacity development at national and regional levels for the provision meteorological, hydrological and climate services to support decision-making for safety of lives, livelihoods and property.

Evolution of WMO Space-based Global Observing System (GOS)

The World Meteorological Organization has a pioneering role in the global action on climate change, as the credit of establishing the Intergovernmental Panel on Climate Change goes to it, with the United Nations Environment Programame (UNEP), in 1988. It performs a huge role in observing and monitoring climate and in providing information and services to the governments. Its structure includes 10- major scientific and technical programmes, 8 Technical Commissions which advise and guide the activities of the programmes and its 6 Regional Associations are involved in implementation. It collects vast data, day in and day out, brings out enormous information and derived products, which are widely available and exchanged freely everyday between its centers and weather services in each country, and between and among countries around the world.

The International Global Observing System (GOS) that has grown substantially since 1961 (Figure 12) and now includes constellations of operational satellites in geostationary and low-Earth orbit, as well as research and development satellites underpins these observations. Since 1993, WMO has issued annual statements on the status of the global climate, which describe climatic conditions, including extreme weather events, and it has provided a historical perspective on the variability and trends that have occurred since the nineteenth century. This information, which is contained in the statements, enhance the scientific understanding of climate variability and the associated impacts that affect the well-being, properties and lives of people around the world.

World Climate Programme (WCP)

The World Climate Programme (WCP) primarily aims at enhancing climate services with adequate focus on user interaction, to facilitate evermore useful applications of climate information to derive optimal socio-economic benefits and thereby underpins the Global Framework for Climate Services (GFCS). The scope of WCP is to determine the physical basis of the climate system that would allow increasingly skilful climate predictions and projections, develop operational structures to provide climate services and to develop and maintain an essential global observing system fully capable of meeting the climate information needs.

World Climate Research Programme

The mission of WCRP is to facilitate analysis and prediction of earth system variability and change for use in an increasing range of practical applications of direct relevance, benefit and value to society.

The overall objectives of the World Climate Research Programme are to determine to what extent climate can be predicted and the extent of human influence on climate.

Global Climate Observing System

The Global Climate Observing System (GCOS) is a WMO-led co-sponsored programme of WMO, the IOC of UNESCO, UNEP and ICSU. The GCOS is built on existing operational and scientific observing, data management and information distribution systems. It is based upon an improved World Weather Watch Global Observing System, the Global Ocean Observing Systems, the Global Terrestrial Observing System, the WMO global observing systems and the maintenance and enhancement of programmes monitoring other key components of the climate system, such as the distribution of important atmospheric constituents (including the Global Atmosphere Watch).

The vision of the GCOS programme is that all users have access to the climate observations, data records and information which they require to address pressing climate-related concerns. GCOS users include individuals, national and international organizations, institutions and agencies. The role of GCOS is to work with partners to ensure the sustained provision of reliable physical, chemical and biological observations and data records for the total climate system – across the atmospheric, oceanic and terrestrial domains, including hydrological and carbon cycles and the cryosphere.

References:

1. World Meteorological Organization- mandates, objectives (http://unfccc.int/files/adaptation/cancun_adaptation_framework/loss_and_damage/application/pdf/wmo.pdf)

2. WMO in Brief – World Meteorological Organization (http://www.wmo.int/pages/about/index_en.html)

Chapter 13

INTERGOVERNMENTAL PANEL ON CLIMATE CHANGE (IPCC)- THE APEX SCIENTIFIC BODY

Scientists have become the bearers of the torch of discovery in our quest for knowledge.

Stephen Hawking

In the chapter 5 it is shown how the knowledge of greenhouse gases evolved since the nineteenth century. During the 1950s, 1960s and 1970s many scientists, through their findings, showed the effect of greenhouse gases. The harmful effects of the increasing greenhouse gas concentrations were manifesting in the form of various aberrations of climate, frequent occurrences of drought, and flooding, increased incidences of hurricanes, increasing frequency and intensity of extreme weather events. In 1979, in response to these happenings and scientific findings the World Meteorological Organization (WMO), the United Nations Environment Programme (UNEP), Food and Agriculture Organization (FAO), UNESCO and the World Health Organization (WHO) organized the first **World Climate Conference**. The deliberations of the conference and the scientific research findings raised alarm of something being wrong with the climate that needed to be thoroughly looked into. The matter was too complex to be effectively handled by the existing UN organizations. It was beyond the scope of the General Practitioner medico; a team of specialists was needed; a pool of very high level expertise in scientific knowledge, environment science and socio-economic field, to be drawn from the world over. Active association of all the countries was needed. Thus, with the initiative of the WMO and UNEP, **the Intergovernmental Panel on Climate Change (IPCC) was established in 1988 to assess the state of existing knowledge about climate change; its science, the environmental economic and social impacts and possible response strategies**. The UN General Assembly in the same year endorsed the action by WMO and UNEP of jointly establishing the IPCC. The IPCC is the apex scientific body in the world as regards the climate change science. It reviews and assesses the most recent scientific, technical and socio-economic information produced worldwide relevant to the understanding of climate change. It does not itself conduct any research nor does it monitor climate related data or parameters. There are other world level specialized agencies in the UN system for that purpose. Today what the world authentically knows about climate change, its magnitude, its impacts, is through the Assessment Reports of the IPCC. It is highest world level authoritative body in the UN system on climate change.

Thousands of scientists from all over the world contribute to the work of the IPCC on a voluntary basis. Review is an essential part of the IPCC process, to ensure an objective and complete assessment of current information. The IPCC aims to reflect a range of views and expertise. The Secretariat coordinates all the IPCC work and liaises with governments. It is supported by WMO and UNEP and hosted at WMO headquarters in Geneva.

The IPCC is an intergovernmental body. It is open to all member countries of the United Nations (UN) and WMO. Currently 195 countries are members of the IPCC. Governments participate in the review process and the plenary sessions, where main decisions about the IPCC work programmes are taken, and reports are accepted, adopted and approved. The IPCC Bureau Members, including the Chair, are also elected during the plenary sessions. Because of its scientific and intergovernmental nature, the IPCC embodies a unique opportunity to provide rigorous and balanced scientific information to decision makers. By endorsing the IPCC reports, governments acknowledge the authority of their scientific content. The work of the organization is therefore policy-relevant and yet policy-neutral, never policy-prescriptive. In December 2007, the IPCC was awarded the Nobel Peace Prize for its efforts to build up and disseminate greater knowledge about man-made climate change.

The Authors

Hundreds of experts are involved on a voluntary basis in the preparation of IPCC reports. Coordinating Lead Authors and Lead Authors for IPCC reports are selected by the relevant Working Group/Task Force Bureau, under general guidance provided by the Session of the Working Group (or by the Panel in case of reports prepared by the Task Force on National Greenhouse Gas Inventories) from among experts listed by governments and participating organizations, and other experts known through their publications and works. None of them is paid by the IPCC.

Review Editors & Expert Reviewers

The role of Review Editors in the IPCC assessment process is to assist the Working Group/Task Force Bureaus in identifying reviewers for the expert review process, to ensure that all substantive expert and government review comments are afforded appropriate consideration by the author teams, and to advise lead authors on how to handle contentious/controversial issues and ensure that genuine controversies are reflected adequately in the text of the Report. There will be two to four Review Editors per chapter and per technical summary of any IPCC assessment.

Expert Reviewers review an IPCC draft report either by invitation or at their own request. IPCC Reports undergo a multi-stage review process Thousands of scientists from all over the world participate in the IPCC review process as expert reviewers.

Structure

Thousands of scientists from all over the world contribute to the work of the IPCC on a voluntary basis as authors, contributors and reviewers. The work of IPCC is guided by a set of principles and procedures. The Panel takes major decisions at Plenary Sessions of government representatives. A central IPCC Secretariat supports the work of the IPCC.

The IPCC is currently organized in 3 Working Groups and a Task Force. They are assisted by Technical Support Units (TSUs), which are hosted and financially supported by the government of the developed country Co-Chair of that Working Group/Task Force. A TSU may also be established to support the IPCC Chair in preparing the Synthesis Report for an assessment report.

The Panel meets in Plenary Sessions at the level of Government Representatives for all member countries. It meets approximately once a year at the plenary level. These Sessions are attended by hundreds of officials and experts from relevant Ministries, Agencies and Research Institutions from Member countries and from observer organizations. Major decisions are taken by the Panel during the Plenary Session.

Writing and Review Process

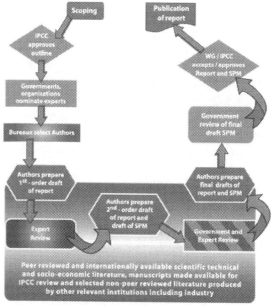

Fig. 13 (IPCC(http://www.ipcc.ch/organization/
organization_procedures.shtml)_

1. Each Report is preceded by a scoping meeting that develops its draft outline. Based on the report of the scoping meeting, the Panel decides whether to prepare a report and agrees on its scope, outline and work plan including schedule and budget.

Authors are chosen from lists drawn up by member governments, observer organizations and the Bureaux (Co-Chairs and Vice-Chairs) of the Working Group or Task Force producing the report. The Bureau of the Working Group or Task Force selects the authors from these lists and other experts known through their publications and work.

The composition of the group of Coordinating Lead Authors and Lead Authors for a chapter, report of summary reflects the range of scientific, technical and socio-economic expertise; geographical representation, ensuring appropriate representation of experts from developing and developed countries and countries with economies in transition; a mixture of experts with and without previous experience in the IPCC; and gender balance. Scientists who are nominated but not selected as authors are invited to register as expert reviewers for the report.

A first draft of the report is prepared by the authors based on available scientific, technical and socio-economic information. The role of the IPCC is to assess all relevant scientific information. Priority is given to peer-reviewed scientific, technical and socio-economic literature. The IPCC recognizes that non-peer reviewed literature, such as reports from governments and industry can be crucial for IPCC assessments, and the appropriate use of such literature expands the breadth and depth of the assessment by including relevant information. Use of this literature brings with it an extra responsibility for the author teams to ensure the quality and validity of cited sources and information.

Review is an essential part of the IPCC process to ensure objective and complete assessment of the current information. In the course of the multi-stage review process- first by experts and then by governments and experts- both expert reviewers and governments are invited to comment on the accuracy and completeness of the scientific, technical and socio-economic content and the overall balance of the drafts. The circulation process among peer and government experts is very wide, with hundreds of scientists looking into the drafts to check the soundness of the scientific information contained in them. The Review Editors of the report (normally two per chapter) make sure that all comments are taken into account by the author teams. Review comments are retained in an open archive on completion of a report.

After the first order draft has been reviewed by experts, authors prepare a second order draft of the report and a first draft of its Summary for Policymakers (SPM). The second order draft of the report and the first draft of the SPM are subject to simultaneous review by both governments and experts. Authors then prepare final drafts of the report and SPM. These are distributed to governments who provide written comments on the revised draft of the SPM before meeting in plenary to approve the SPM and accept the report.

The Assessment Reports of the IPCC have three parts, each one of the respective group. It includes a Summary for

Policy Makers (SPM), which is a component of the Report. It provides a policy-relevant but policy neutral summary of that Report.

Working Group I, deals with "The Physical Science Basis of Climate Change",

Working Group II covers "Climate Change Impacts, Adaptation and Vulnerability"

and Working Group III concerns with "Mitigation of Climate Change".

Synthesis Report contains summary of the main findings of all the three reports.

The IPCC have so far produced five Assessment Reports, besides a number of special reports, technical papers, guidelines etc.

The Fifth Assessment Report (AR5).

WG I: The Physical Science Basis – 30 September 2013, Summary for Policymakers published 27 September 2013.

WG II: Impacts, Adaptation and Vulnerability – 31 March 2014.

WG III: Mitigation of Climate Change – 11 April 2014.

AR5 Synthesis Report (SYR) – 2 November 2014.

The AR5 provides an update of knowledge on the scientific, technical and socio-economic aspects of climate change.

Impacts of the Assessment Reports of the IPCC

1. The First Assessment Report (FAR,1990), in three parts, viz. Scientific Assessment, Impacts Assessment, Response Strategies, Emission Scenarios. It was a first report of the authoritative body set up at world level. This report, besides, throwing light on various scientific aspects of the phenomenon of climate change, had an impact in defining the content of the UNFCCC.

2. The Second Assessment Report (SAR, 1996) provided more scientific details of the phenomenon and was largely influential in defining the provisions of the Kyoto Protocol.

3. The Third Assessment Report (TAR, 2001) focused attention on the impacts of climate change and the need for adaptation.

4. The Fourth Assessment Report (AR4, 2007) informed the decision on the ultimate objective (2^0C) and provided a strong basis for a post Kyoto Protocol agreement.

5. The Fifth Assessment Report (AR5, 2013-14) has influenced review of the 2^0 C objective, in the context for preparing post-Durban 2015 agreement, i.e. successor to Kyoto Protocol and future course of action.

References:

1. IPCC (http://www.ipccich)

2. Facts/How the IPCC works (www.ipccfacts.org/history.html)

3. IPCC- Intergovernmental Panel on Climate Change (http://www.ipcc.ch/organization/organization_procedures.shtml)_

Chapter 14

UNITED NATIONS FRAMEWORK CONVENTION ON CLIMATE CHANGE (UNFCCC) AND THE CONFERENCE OF PARTIES (COP)

The IPCC was established to objectively review and assess the body of scientific, technical and socio-economic literature for understanding human induced climate change, and to present options for adaptation and mitigation, there was a need of a forum or body of nations to act together and deliberate upon the action to be taken to tackle the threat, and take decisions collectively. The UN General Assembly established an Intergovernmental Negotiations Committee in 1992, to draft a framework convention on climate change. (The word 'convention" stands for an official agreement between countries). The Committee produced the text of the Framework Convention as a report following its meeting in New York from April 30 to May, 1992. It was opened for signature on May 9, 1992. The convention drafted by the INC was adopted in the UN Conference on Environment and Development (UNCED) styled as Earth Summit, held in Rio de Janerio, where it was signed in June 1992. To quote from UNFCCC itself – In 1992, countries joined an international treaty the UNFCCC, **"to co-operatively consider what they could do to limit average global temperature increases and the resulting climate change, and to cope with whatever impacts were, by then, inevitable."** It came into force from 21 March, 1994. It has 194 parties. It is aimed at stabilizing greenhouse gas concentrations in the atmosphere at a level that would prevent dangerous anthropogenic interface with the climate system commonly believed to be around 2^0 C above the pre-industrial global average temperature.

UNFCCC- the body, Parties, objectives and working.

The UNFCCC is an international environment treaty (also termed as multi-lateral environment agreement) - a treaty among nations called Parties, as such it is also an international decision making body of 194 Parties. The UNFCCC is also the name of the United Nations Secretariat charged with supporting the operation the Convention, with its office in Bonn, Germany.

To pursue its objectives its Parties i.e. the signatory nations-

- Gather and share information of greenhouse gas emissions, national policies and best practices;
- Launch national strategies for addressing greenhouse gas emissions and measures for adapting the expected impacts, including the

financial and technological support to developing countries.

- Cooperate in preparing for adaptation to the impacts of climate change.

Commitments under the UNFCCC

The UNFCCC sets an overall framework for international efforts to tackle the challenge of climate change. Parties to the Convention agreed to a number of commitments to address climate change:

- ❖ To develop and periodically submit national reports containing information on the greenhouse gas emissions of that Party and describing the steps it has taken and plans to take to implement the Convention.
- ❖ To put in place national programmes and measures to control emissions and to adapt to the impacts of climate change.
- ❖ To promote the development and use of climate-friendly technologies and the sustainable management of forests and other ecosystems.

Additional commitments for the industrialized countries called Annex I Parties:

- ❖ Undertake policies measures with the specific aim of returning their greenhouse gas emissions to 1990 levels by 2000. (*Under the Kyoto Protocol, which is an update of the Convention, 37 Annex I Parties have specific binding emission targets to be achieved in the 2008-2012 commitment period, to*

*reduce emissions from these Parties by about 5%
from 1990 levels)*

❖ Provide more frequent and more detailed national
reports and must separately provide yearly reports
on their national greenhouse gas emissions.

❖ Promote and facilitate the transfer of climate
friendly technologies to developing countries and
to countries with economies in transition.

Its meetings are called **Conference of Parties (COP)**
which is held annually. One hundred and ninety five
nations working on the huge complex global problem as
climate change will require supporting mechanism. As
such besides its secretariat, it has set-up Subsidiary Body
of Implementation (SBI) and another Subsidiary Body for
Scientific and Technological Aspects (SBSTA). These bodies
give advice to the COPs, and each has a specific mandate.
The SBI gives advice to the COPs on all matters concerning
the implementation of the Convention. The SBSTA's task is
to provide the COP with advice on scientific, technological
and methodological matters.

Its Principles

A key element of the UNFCCC that enjoins its members is to
protect the climate system **"on the basis of equality and
in accordance with their common but differentiated
responsibilities and respective capabilities"** The
principle is well thought out and is very meaningful. It
implies firstly the common responsibility of each of
the Parties to protect the environment at their level. It
also includes the need to take into account the different
circumstances and each Party's contribution to the

problem and its ability to prevent, reduce and control the threat. Another key element of its approach is the **'polluter pays principle'**, i.e. the Party responsible for producing pollution (emission) is responsible for paying the damage done to the natural environment.

The UNFCCC treaty in itself does not set any mandatory limits of greenhouse gas emissions for individual nations, and does not contain any enforcement provisions But the scheme of the things is that the treaty included provisions for updates called "protocols (the word "protocol is used in the sense of an extra part that would be added to the original treaty).The principal update of the UNFCCC is the **Kyoto Protocol,** which lays down mandatory limits for greenhouse gas emissions. One of the achievements of UNFCCC was to establish a greenhouse inventory as a benchmark and count of greenhouse as emissions and removals. Signatory nations are required to regularly submit the account of progress.

The Convention divides countries into three main groups according to differing commitments:

Annex I Parties include the industrialized countries that were members of the OECD (Organisation for Economic Co-operation and Development) in 1992, plus countries with economies in transition (the EIT Parties), including the Russian Federation, the Baltic States, and several Central and Eastern European States[A]. The Parties are: Australia, Austria, Belarus, Belgium, Bulgaria, Canada, Croatia, Cyprus, Czech Republic, Denmark, Estonia, European Union, Finland, France, Germany, Greece, Hungary, Iceland, Ireland, Italy Japan, Latvia, Liechtenstein, Lithuania, Luxembourg, Malta, Monaco, Netherlands, New

Zealand, Norway, Poland, Portugal, Romania, the Russian Federation, Slovakia, Slovenia, Spain, Sweden, Switzerland, Turkey, Ukraine, the United Kingdom of Great Britain and Northern Ireland, and the United States of America. (Source: http://unfccc.int/parties_and_observers/parties/annex_i/items/2774.php).

Annex II Parties consist of the OECD members of Annex I, but not the EIT Parties. They are required to provide financial resources to enable developing countries to undertake emissions reduction activities under the Convention and to help them adapt to adverse effects of climate change. In addition, they have to "take all practicable steps" to promote the development and transfer of environmentally friendly technologies to EIT Parties and developing countries. Funding provided by Annex II Parties is channeled mostly through the Convention's financial mechanism. These countries include Australia, Austin, Belgium, Canada, Denmark, European Economic Community, Finland, France, Germany, Greece, Iceland, Ireland, Italy, Japan, Luxembourg, Netherlands, New Zealand, Norway, Portugal, Spain, Sweden, Switzerland, Turkey, United Kingdom of Great Britain and Northern Ireland and the United States of America. (List of Parties from http: //unfccc.int/cop3/fccc/climate/annex2.htm).

Non Annex Countries: Developing countries (Rest of the above)

Annex B countries / parties: Group of countries that have agreed to a target for their greenhouse gas emissions, including all the Annex I countries (as amended in 1998), excluding Turkey and Belarus.

Conference of Parties

The signatory nations of UNFCCC meet annually in the international conference called Conference of Parties. Since 2005 these conferences are held in conjunction with the Meetings of Parties of the Kyoto Protocol, and in such meeting (CMPs) the nations that have not signed the Kyoto Protocol are allowed to participate with the Protocol related meetings as observers. The functions of the CMP relating to the Protocol are similar to those carried out by the COP for the Convention.

Following is the list of the Conference of Parties:

1. COP 1- Berlin, Germany, 1995(28 March to 7 April).
2. COP 2 - Geneva, Switzerland, 1996 (8 to 19 July).
3. COP 3 - Kyoto, Japan, 1997 (1 to 10 December).
4. COP 4 - Buenos Aires, Argentina 1998 (2 to 13 November).
5. COP 5 - Bonn, Germany 1999 (October 25 to 5 November).
6. COP6 - Hague, Netherland, 2000 (13 - 25 November).
7. Part II of the sixth COP -Bonn, 2001 (17 --27 July).
8. COP 7 - Marrakech, Morocco, 2001 (29 October – 10 November).
9. COP 8 - New Delhi, India 2002 (23 October to 1 November). COP 9 - Milan, Italy 2003 (1 - 12 December).
10. COP 10 Buenos Aires, 2004 (6 - 17 December).
11. COP11 Montreal, Canada 2005 (28 November to 11 December).
12. COP 12 - Nairobi, Kenya 2006 (3 – 15 December)
13. COP 13 - Bali, Indonesia 2007 (3-14 December).
14. COP 14 - Poznan, Poland 2008 (1 to 12 December).

15. COP 15 - Copenhagen, Denmark 2009 (7 to 18 December).
16. COP 16 - Cancun, Mexico 2010 (29 November to 10 December).
17. COP 17 - Durban, South Africa 2011 (28 November to 9 December).
18. COP 18 - Doha, Qatar 2012 (26 November to 8 December).
19. COP 19, Warsaw, Poland (11-23 November, 2013).
20. COP 20. Lima (Peru) (1-14 December, 2014).
21. COP 21 Paris (30 November -11 December, 2015).

References:

1. World Meteorological Organization (www.int/pages/themes/climate/international_unfccc.php)

2. UNFCCC and the COP Climate Leaders (www.climate leaders.org)

3. A Brief overview of Conferences (http://unfccc.int/documentation/decisions/items/2964.php)

4. Wikipedia, the free encyclopedia

5. Doha Climate Conference (http://unfccc.int/meetings/doha-net)

6. Wikipedia, free Encyclopedia.

Chapter 15

KYOTO PROTOCOL

In an earlier chapter we have seen that the United Nations Framework Convention on Climate Change (UNFCCC) is an international treaty aimed at stabilizing greenhouse gas (GHG) concentrations in the atmosphere at a level that would prevent dangerous anthropogenic interference with the climate. It was also mentioned that the treaty itself sets no mandatory limits on greenhouse gas emissions. Rather, it included provisions for updates (called "protocols") that would set mandatory emission limits.

In the third Conference of Parties (COP-3) held in Kyoto, Japan, between 1-11 December, 1997 the Parties entered into an international agreement linked to the UNFCCC. Known as **Kyoto Protocol**, which, *inter alia*, sets binding obligations on the 37 industrialized countries and the European Union to reduce their anthropogenic greenhouse gas emissions by at least 5% below 1990 levels in the commitment period 2008-2012. It came into force from 16 February 2005. It also laid down a road map of action. It would be appropriate to mention the distinction between the Convention and the Protocol. The Convention *encourages* the industrialized nations to stabilize GHG emissions; the Protocol *commits* them to do so. It is now extended from 2013 to 2020, when the new agreement to be finalized in 2015, is expected to come into force.

Second Commitment Period

The Doha Amendment is an amendment to the Kyoto Protocol that was adopted by the Conference of Parties serving as the meeting of the Parties to the Protocol (CMP) on 8 December, 2012 in Doha, Qatar. This establishes the second commitment period of the Kyoto Protocol, which began on 1 January, 2013 and will end on 31 December, 2020.

There are many details of the Kyoto Protocol. A few major contents are mentioned in this chapter.

- **Binding commitments** for the Annex I Parties (listed below). The main feature of the Protocol is that it established legally binding commitments to reduce their anthropogenic greenhouse gas emissions by at least 5% below 1990 levels in the commitment period 2008-2012 for Annex I Parties and the European Union. The commitments are based on the Berlin Mandate, which was a part of the UNFCCC negotiations leading up to the Protocol.
- **Implementation**. In order to meet the objectives of the Protocol, Annex I Parties are required to prepare policies and measures for the reduction of greenhouse gas emissions in their respective countries. In addition, they are required to increase the absorption of these gases and utilize all mechanisms available, such as Joint Implementation, the Clean Development

Mechanism and Emissions Trading, in order to be rewarded with credits that would allow more greenhouse gas emissions at home.

- Minimizing Impacts on developing countries by establishing an adaptation fund for climate change.
- Accounting, reporting and review in order to ensure the integrity of the Protocol.
- **Compliance.** Establishing a Compliance Committee to enforce compliance with the commitments under the Protocol.

Ireland, and the United States of America.

THE AGREEMENT

The Annex I countries which have ratified the Protocol have committed themselves to reduce their greenhouse gas emission levels by about 5% below their 1990 levels in the time frame of 2008-2012. They were to do this by allocating reduced annual allowances to the major operators within their borders. These operators can only exceed their allocations if they buy emission allowances (emissions trading explained here separately) or offset their excesses through a mechanism that is agreed by all parties to the UNFCCC. Developing countries are not required to reduce emission levels unless developed countries supply enough funding and technology. This was done to serve three purposes:

➢ To avoid restriction on their industrial capacity that is linked to development.

> ➤ To be allowed to sell their emission credits to nations whose operators have difficulty in meeting their emission targets.
> ➤ To get money and technologies for low carbon investments from Annex II countries. It is also provided that developing countries may volunteer to become Annex I countries when they are sufficiently developed.

Greenhouse gas emissions to be reduced

The targets of reducing the emissions apply to the four greenhouse gases viz. carbon dioxide (CO_2), methane (CH_4), nitrous oxide (N_2O), sulphur hexafluoride (SF_6) and two groups of gases – hydrofluorocarbons (HFC_s) and Perfluorocarbons (PFCs). These six gases are converted into CO_2 equivalents in determining reductions in emissions. These six gases are in addition to the industrial gases, chlorofluorocarbon (CFC's) which are ozone depleting gases.

Adoption and Ratification of Protocol

The Protocol was initially adopted on 11 December, 1997 in Kyoto, Japan. The detailed rules for implementation of the Protocol were adopted at COP 7 in Marrakech. The Protocol entered into force effective 16 February 2005. As of now (2014) 191 countries have signed and ratified the Protocol. The only signatory not to have ratified is the United States of America. Other UN member countries which did not ratify the Protocol are Afghanistan, Andorra and South Sudan. In December 2011 Canada withdrew from the Protocol. The

Protocol's first commitment period was up to 2012 (since expired and continued from 2013 to 2020) when a new international framework needs to have been negotiated and ratified that can deliver the stringent emission reductions as the IPCC has clearly indicated, are needed.

Annex B Countries: The term Annex I, Annex II, countries are part of the UNFCCC. Since Kyoto Protocol is linked the UNFCCC, these terms are used in the Protocol. However, the Protocol also used the term **Annex B Countries**, which includes the countries that have agreed to a target for their greenhouse gas emissions, including almost all the Annex I countries except Turkey and Belarus. At the time of adoption of the Protocol the European Union was not formed, as such each of the European country was included as a separate Party.

These countries are European Union (which is a union of 15 countries), Bulgaria, Czech Republic, Estonia, Latvia, Liechtenstein, Lithuania, Monaco, Hungary, Japan, Poland, Croatia, New Zealand, Russian Federation, Ukrain, Norway, Australia, Iceland. The USA did not ratify and Canada withdrew[3]. (http://unfccc.int/kyoto_protocol/items/3145.php).

Greater responsibility of developed countries

The Protocol recognized that developed countries are principally responsible for the current high levels of GHG emissions in the atmosphere as a result of more than 150 years of industrial activity. The Protocol places a heavier burden on developed nations under the principle of *"common but differentiated responsibilities", also stated as "polluter pays".*

The Protocol Mechanism:

1. Under the Protocol, the countries must meet their
    targets primarily through national measures.
    However, the Protocol provides flexibility
    mechanisms by offering them additional means
    of meeting their targets by way of three market
    based mechanisms. These are:-

    a) International Emissions Trading (IET) also
        known as "the carbon market"
    b) Clean Development Mechanism (CDM)
    c) Joint Implementation (JI)

2. Monitoring Emission Targets:

    a) Under the Protocol, countries' actual emissions
        are to be monitored and precise records of the
        trades carried out are to be kept.
    b) Registry Systems. There is a Registry system
        to keep track and record of transactions by the
        Parties under the mechanisms. The UN Climate
        Change Secretariat, based in Bonn, Germany,
        keeps an *international transaction log* to verify
        that the transactions are consistent with the
        rules of the Protocol.
    c) Reporting. This is done by the Parties by way
        of annual emission inventories and national
        reports under the Protocol at regular intervals.
    d) Compliance. The compliance system
        ensures that the Parties are meeting their
        commitments. It helps them to meet their
        commitments, if they have problem doing so.

e) Adaptation. Like the UNFCCC the Protocol has mechanism to assist countries in adapting to the adverse effects of climate change. It facilitates the development of techniques that can help increase resilience to the impacts of climate change.

f) Adaptation Fund: This fund was established to finance adaptation projects and programmes in development countries that are Parties to the Protocol.

The Fund is financed mainly with a share of CDM project activities. The Flexibility Mechanisms are briefly explained as under:

Emission Trading:

Parties with commitments under the Kyoto Protocol (Annex B Parties) have accepted targets for limiting or reducing emissions. These targets are expressed as levels of allowed emissions or "assigned amount units" (AAUs). Emissions trading as set out in Article 17 of the Kyoto Protocol, allows countries that have emission units to spare-emissions permitted them but not used- to sell this excess capacity to countries that are over their targets. Thus, a new commodity was created in the form of emission reductions or removals.

Under the Kyoto Protocol the Annex I Parties are allowed to use International Emission Trading. Under the 5 year compliance period from 2008 to 2012 (and now in the extended period up to 2020) the nations that emit less than their quota will be able to sell assigned amount units to the nations that exceed their quotas.

Clean Development Mechanism

The Clean Development Mechanism (CDM) is one of the flexibility mechanisms, provided under Article 12 of the Kyoto Protocol. It enables the developing countries to participate in joint greenhouse gas mitigation projects. The Annex I countries, who are required to reduce greenhouse gas emissions below their 1990 levels, can meet their reduction commitments in a flexible and cost effective way. It allows public or private sector entities in the Annex I countries to invest in greenhouse gas mitigation projects in developing countries. In return, the investing parties receive credits or certified emission reductions (CER) which they can use to meet their targets under the Protocol. This serves two purposes. The investors profit from CDM projects by obtaining reductions at costs lower than in their own countries; the gains to the developing host countries, are in the form of finance, technology and sustainable development funds. It is necessary that a CDM project must provide emission reductions that are *additional* to what would otherwise have occurred. This includes afforestation and re-forestation project. The projects must lead to real measurable and long term GHG reductions.

Approval to the projects is given by the Designated National Authorities. The mechanism is overseen by the CDM Executive Board. Since 2006, more than 4957 projects are registered anticipated to produce 1,055,653,877 certified emission reductions.

Joint Implementation

Joint Implementation (JI), as set forth in Article 6 of the Kyoto Protocol, is one of the three flexible mechanisms to help the Annex I countries having binding greenhouse gas emission targets, to meet their obligations. The mechanism allows a country with an emission reduction or limitation commitment (as under Annex B – Annex B contains commitments given to Annex I parties) to earn emission reduction units (ERUs) from the emission reduction or emission removal projects in another Annex B party, each equivalent to one tone of CO2, which can be counted towards meeting the Protocol target. (Thus JI is between two countries who are Annex I parties. The main difference between the CDM and JI lies in their application as JI projects can only be hosted by the countries with emission reduction or limitation commitments.

CARBON CREDITS

Credit means something earned, something added to one's account. The words "certain amount of carbon dioxide" mean one metric ton of carbon dioxide or its multiples. Carbon dioxide includes its equivalent greenhouse gases.. Thus, a carbon credit is created when one metric ton of carbon dioxide (or its equivalent) is prevented from entering the atmosphere.

The certificate mentioned above has a certain monetary value. Internationally these are termed as Certified Carbon Reductions, Emission Reduction Units or Verified / Certified Emission Reductions. Only the projects that carry the seal of approval from the UNFCCC are eligible for carbon credits. The UNFCCC has created methodologies and also have organizations that approve, certify and register projects under the CDM and JI. To counter the greenhouse gas emissions, which are adding to global warming, and as provided under the Clean Development Mechanism of the Kyoto Protocol, a developed country can take up a greenhouse gas reduction project activity in a developing country where the cost of such projects is usually lower. The developed country gets carbon credits equal to the emissions reduced for meeting (offsetting) its emission reduction targets, while the developing country will receive the capital and clean technology to implement the project. One carbon credit equals one ton of carbon dioxide (or other greenhouse carbon dioxide equivalent gas) prevented. These credits are bought and sold on international carbon credit exchanges.

Under the JI emitters in the developed countries (Annex I countries) are allowed to purchase carbon credits via project based transactions implemented in another developed country or a country with economy is transition. The carbon credits from JI projects are referred to as

Paris Accord-Successor to Kyoto Protocol

During the 21st Conference of Parties held in Paris from 30 November to 12 December, 2016, an accord has been reached wherein nearly every country has conveyed its action plan to bring down the emission levels.

References:

1. UNFCCC (www.unfccc.int/kyotoprotocol)

2. UNFCCC (Unfccc.int/files/Kyoto_protocol/ doha/_amendment/application)

3. World Bank – Carbon Finance Unit (web.worldbank. org/wbsite/externaltopics.env

4. By Joseph E. Aldy, Scott Barrett and Robert N. Stovins (www.sciencedirect.com)

Chapter 16

ADAPTATION TO CLIMATE CHANGE

'Adaptation' is a term of biology, sociology, psychology and now a key word in the human response to climate change. In biology it is defined as: *Adjustment in natural or human systems in response to actual of expected climate stimuli or their effects, which moderates harm or exploits beneficial opportunities[1].* Throughout the ages, man has adapted himself to changes in weather, climate and all other adversities. It is in man's nature. It is as simple as we wear woolen clothes in winter or use a raincoat in rainy season- that is adaptation. Since we are concerned here with adaptation to climate change, it may not be as simple as wearing woolen clothes. It is specific and requires many efforts at individual, community, national and international level.

The IPCC defines Adaptation as[2]: "Adjustment in natural or *human systems* to a new or changing environment. Adaptation to *climate change* refers to adjustment in natural or human systems in response to actual or expected climate *stimuli* or their effects, which moderates harm or exploits beneficial opportunities. Various types of adaptation can be distinguished, including anticipatory and reactive adaptation, private and public adaptation, and autonomous and planned adaptation." Every new assessment report of the IPCC tells us of more damages and potential dire consequences to human and ecosystems of the earth than what were mentioned in the previous consequences (See Summary of AR5-WGII). Adaptation necessitates taking a range of activities to reduce vulnerability and build resilience in almost all the key sectors – health, water, agriculture, human settlements. It will require new and improved technologies and financing initiatives at all levels as a part of collective efforts to address climate change.

Adaptation and sustainable development

Alongside of response to climate change, the world has realized the significance of **sustainable development** economic challenges faced by humanity[3]. Climate change impacts on all aspects of sustainable development. Future vulnerability depends not only on climate change, but also on development pathways. Sustainable development can reduce vulnerability, in addition to its other immense benefits. The implementation of adaptation needs to be integrated into national and international sustainable development priorities, as well as into national and sectoral development plans.

Steps for effective implementation strategies at national level include[4]:

- Enhancement of the scientific basis for decision-making.

- Strengthening methods and tools for the assessment of adaptation.
- Education, training and public awareness on adaptation, including for youth.
- Individual and institutional capacity-building.
- Technology development and transfer; and promotion of local coping strategies.
- Appropriate legislation and regulatory frameworks, which promote adaptive-friendly action.
- An adaptive planning process that covers different time-scales and levels (e.g. national, regional) and sectors.

Using climate change, including adaptation, as a driver to undertake activities with multiple benefits can catalyze progress in achieving a country's sustainable development goals.

Adaptation Options

Adaptation is a generic term, under which a large number of specific course of action come. A few adaptation options as summarized in the UNFCCC Fact Sheet are as under[5].

- Behavioural change at the individual level, such as the sparing use of water in times of drought.
- Technological and engineering options such as increased sea defenses or flood-proof houses.
- Risk management and reduction strategies such as early warning systems for extreme events.
- Promotion of adaptive management strategies.

- Development of financial instruments such as insurance schemes.
- Promotion of ecosystem management practices, such as biodiversity conservation to reduce the impacts of climate change on people, e.g. by conserving and restoring mangroves to protect people from storms.

UNFCCC and Adaptation of Climate Change

The purpose of setting the United Nations Framework Convention on Climate Change is *to co-operatively consider what they (nations) could to limit average global temperature increases and the resulting climate change, and to cope with whatever impacts were, by then, inevitable.* As such the theme of adaptation permeates throughout the text of UNFCCC.

- ❖ The UNFCCC provides the basis for concerted international action to mitigate climate change to adapt to its impact. Its provisions are far sighted, innovative and firmly embedded in the concept of sustainable development[6]
- ❖ "All the parties shall take climate change considerations into account, to the extent feasible, in their relevant social, economic and environmental policies and actions, and employ appropriate methods for example, impact assessment formulated and determined nationally, with a view to minimizing adverse effects on the economy, on public health and on the quality of environment, of projects and measures undertaken by them to mitigate or adapt to climate change". (UNFCCC Article 4.1f)

Funding for Adaptation[7]

Adaptation to climate change needs huge funds on sustained basis so that countries can plan for and implement adaptation plans and projects. Funding is required for all developing countries to develop national adaptation plans and for these to exist at all levels: local, sub-national and national. Many estimates for financing adaptations actions have been produced in recent time. While it is difficult to ascertain their accuracy given that they involve future costs, it is safe to say that funding requirements for adaptation are likely to run to several billions of dollars annually. Current **Official Development Assistance***(ODA) is insufficient to cover the adaptation needs. According to the UNFCCC, it is critical that start-up funding for adaptation actions in developing countries, as laid down in the **Copenhagen Accord**#(COP 15-December 2009),be made available to address the most urgent adaptation needs.

Current efforts under the UNFCCC[8]

- It is critical that the implementation of adaptation be brought forward on the policy agendas.
- Developing countries need to receive increased and sustained assistance to adapt to the impacts of climate change.
- The climate change regime has to deliver sustained and sufficient funding for the implementation of large-scale adaptation initiatives to prevent funding being largely limited to 'reactive funding', e.g. short-term emergency relief. Reactive funding would be unsupportive of sustainable development

approaches and be very costly. (It is estimated that one US dollar invested in anticipatory measures can save up to 97 US dollars in future relief costs.)

- Foster appropriate enabling environments to ensure effective and efficient provision of capacity-building, technology and funding.

National Adaptation Programmes of Action (NAPAs) are currently an option for the Least Developed Countries and provide a rigorous assessment of urgent adaptation needs in LDCs. Significant support from the international community is needed to implement the projects identified in the NAPAs, such as early-warning systems, disaster risk reduction, improving food security and water resource management. As of October, 2010 donor countries have made contributions and pledges to the LDC Fund of around USD 292 million[9].

The five year **Nairobi Work Programme** (2005-10) on impacts, vulnerability and adaptation to climate change had the objective of assisting all the countries in understanding and assessing impacts, vulnerability and adaptation and making informed decisions on practical adaptation actions and measures to respond to climate change on a sound scientific, technical and socio-economic basis, taking into account current and future climate change and variability. It provides a structured framework for knowledge sharing and collaboration among Parties and organizations. The Programme has been successful in fulfilling its objective and achieving its expected outcomes, in particular, the programme has proved to be an important knowledge-sharing and learning platform on adaptation and effective mechanism for enhancing cooperation among a wide range of adaptation stakeholders and for catalyzing adaptation actions in all regions and sectors[10].

As part of the **Cancun Adaptation Framework**[11]@ (COP 16-2010)

Parties established the Adaptation Committee to promote the implementation of enhanced action on adaptation in a coherent manner under the Convention, inter alia, through the following functions:

1. Providing technical support and guidance to the Parties.
2. Sharing of relevant information, knowledge, experience and good practices.
3. Promoting synergy and strengthening engagement with national, regional and international organizations, centres and networks.
4. Providing information and recommendations, drawing on adaptation good practices, for consideration of COP when providing guidance on means to incentivize the implementation of adaptation actions, including finance, technology and capacity-building.
5. Considering information communicated by Parties on their monitoring and review of adaptation actions, support provided and received.

The Adaptation Fund

The Adaptation Fund was established to finance concrete adaptation projects and programmes in developing countries that Parties to the Kyoto Protocol take up. The

Adaptation Fund is financed with a share of proceeds from Clean Development Mechanism (CDM) project activities and funds from other sources. The share of proceeds amounts to 2% of certified emission reductions (CER) issued for a CDM project activity. The Fund has so far, 2010-2013, dedicated more than 190 million US dollars[12].

References:

1. UNFCCC Glossary of terms. (.http://unfccc.int/essential_background/glossary/items/3666.php)

2. IPCC-Glossary of Terms-Annex B to the TAR (www.ipcc.ch/pdf/glossary/tar)

3. Wikipedia, the free encyclopedia.

4. UNFCCC Fact Sheet-The need for adaptation (http://unfccc.int/press/fact_sheets/items/4985.php)

5. *Ibid*

6. Climate Change: Impacts, Vulnerabilities and Adaptation in Developing Countries (http://unfccc.int/resource/docs/publications/impacts)

7. UNFCCC Fact Sheet: The need for Adaptation, *op.cit*

8. UNFCCC Fact Sheet: The need for Adaptation, *op.cit*

9. UNFCCC Fact Sheet: The need for Adaptation, *op.cit*

10. UNFCCC Fact Sheet: The need for Adaptation, *op.cit*

11. UNFCCC Adaptation Committee (http://unfccc.int/
adaptation/groups_committees/adaptation_committee)

12. UNFCCC Fact Sheet: The need for Adaptation, *op, cit*

*Flows of official financing administered with the promotion of the economic development and welfare of developing countries as the main objective, and which are concessional in character with a grant element of at least 25 percent (using a fixed 10 percent rate of discount).w. — OECD, *Glossary of Statistical Terms* – Wikipedia.

The Copenhagen Accord, inter alia, states that "enhanced action and international cooperation on **adaptation** is urgently required to... reduce] vulnerability and build.. resilience in developing countries, especially in those that are particularly vulnerable, especially least developed countries (LDCs), small island developing states (SIDS) and Africa" and agrees that "developed countries shall provide adequate, predictable and sustainable financial resources, technology and capacity-building to support the implementation of adaptation action in developing countries"-Wikipedia.

@Parties adopted the Cancun Adaptation Framework (CAF) as part of the Cancun Agreements at the 2010 Climate Change Conference in Cancun, Mexico (COP 16/ CMP 6). In the Agreements, Parties affirmed that adaptation must be addressed with the same level of priority as mitigation. The CAF is the result of three years of negotiations on adaptation under the AWG-LCA that had followed the adoption of the Bali Action Plan at the 2007 Climate Change Conference in Bali, Indonesia (COP 13/ CMP 3).-Wikipedia.

Chapter 17

MITIGATION OF CLIMATE CHANGE

Climate Change Mitigation refers to efforts to reduce or prevent emission of greenhouse gases. Mitigation can mean using new technologies and renewable energies, making older equipment more energy efficient, or changing management practices or consumer behavior. It can be as complex as a plan for a new city or as a simple as improvements to a cook stove design. Efforts underway around the world range from high-tech subway systems to bicycling paths and walkways. Protecting natural carbon sinks like forests and oceans, or creating new sinks through silviculture or green agriculture are also elements of mitigation[1]. UNEP (http://www.unep. org/climatechange/mitigation)

From the above quotation it is seen that mitigation involves a process of curbing greenhouse gas emissions from human activities, like emissions from fossil fuels as well as deforestation with a view to stabilize greenhouse gas concentrations at a safe level. Positively, it would involve increasing forest cover, agro-forestry and tree planting in cities so as to sequester carbon dioxide through these natural sinks. This requires huge efforts involving technological change and substitution that reduce resource inputs and emissions per unit of output. Thus mitigation means implementing policies to reduce greenhouse gas missions and enhance sinks.

Mitigation is essential to meet the UNFCCC's objective of stabilizing GHG concentrations in the atmosphere. The Convention[2], *inter alia*, requires all Parties by taking into account their responsibilities and capabilities, to formulate and implement programmes containing measures to mitigate climate change.

- Also requires all Parties to develop and periodically update national inventories of GHG emissions and removals.
- Commits all Parties to promote and cooperate in the development, application and diffusion of climate friendly technologies.
- Requires developed countries to adopt national policies and measures to limit GHG emissions and protect and enhance sinks and reservoirs.
- States that the extent to which developing countries will implement their commitments will depend on financial resources and transfer of technology.
- Kyoto Protocol operationalizes the Convention by committing industrialized countries to limit greenhouse gas emissions. The clean development mechanism (CDM) under the Protocol has been an important avenue of action for the developing countries to implement project activities that reduce emissions and enhance sinks.
- Developing countries are encouraged to contribute to mitigation actions in the forest sector by undertaking activities relating to reducing emissions from deforestation and

forest degradation, conservation of forest carbon stock, sustainable management of forests and enhancement forest stocks (REDD+).

Sector-wise contribution of greenhouse gas emissions and relevant technology and policy[3]:

There are six major areas from where greenhouse gas emissions have risen and are rising, namely,

1. GHG emissions, largely carbon dioxide (CO_2) from the combustion of fossil fuels, have risen dramatically since the pre-industrial times. Globally, energy related CO_2 emissions have risen 145-fold since 1850—from 200 million tons to 29 billion tons a year—and are projected to rise another 54 percent by 2030.

2. Deforestation is estimated to have been the cause 17% of annual greenhouse gas emissions.

3. Agriculture contributes about 14% of greenhouse gas emissions mainly methane and nitrous oxide through use of chemical fertilizers. Livestock accounts 30% of the methane emissions from human activities.

4. Industry contributes about 19% of greenhouse gas emissions.

5. Power supply accounts for about 21% of these emissions.

6. Buildings, waste are other sources of greenhouse gas emissions.

Economics of Mitigation: The UNEP is very vocal when it enjoins the countries to act on mitigation of climate change, when it says[4]:

"The benefits of strong and early action to curb green house gas emissions and mitigate the effects of climate change far outweigh the economic cost of not acting. Hundreds of millions of people around the world could suffer hunger, water shortages and coastal flooding as the world warms. "Our actions now and over the coming decades could create risks of major disruption to economic depression of the first half of the 20th century. And it will be difficult or impossible to reverse these changes. Therefore, prompt and strong action is clearly warranted.

"The world does not need to choose between averting climate change and promoting growth and development. Changes in energy technologies and in the structure of economies have created opportunities to decouple growth from greenhouse gas emissions. Indeed, ignoring climate change will eventually damage economic growth."

Carbon Capture and Storage

According to the proponents of this technology, carbon capture and storage can go a long way in mitigation of greenhouse gas emissions.

According to the Carbon Capture and Storage Association[5], "Carbon Capture and Storage (CCS) is a technology that can capture up to 90% of the carbon dioxide (CO_2) emissions produced from the use of fossil fuels in electricity generation and industrial processes, preventing the carbon dioxide from entering the atmosphere.

"Furthermore, the use of CCS with renewable biomass is one of the few carbon abatement technologies that can be used in a 'carbon-negative' mode – actually taking carbon dioxide out of the atmosphere.

"The CCS chain consists of three parts; capturing the carbon dioxide, transporting the carbon dioxide, and securely storing the carbon dioxide emissions, underground in depleted oil and gas fields or deep saline aquifer formations.

"First, capture technologies allow the separation of carbon dioxide from gases produced in electricity generation and industrial processes by one of three methods: pre-combustion capture, post-combustion capture and oxyfuel combustion.

"Carbon dioxide is then transported by pipeline or by ship for safe storage. Millions of tonnes of carbon dioxide are already transported annually for commercial purposes by road tanker, ship and pipelines. The U.S. has four decades of experience of transporting carbon dioxide by pipeline for enhanced oil recovery projects.

"The carbon dioxide is then stored in carefully selected geological rock formation that are typically located several kilometers below the earth's surface.

"At every point in the CCS chain, from production to storage, industry has at its disposal a number of process technologies that are well understood and have excellent health and safety records. The commercial deployment of CCS will involve the widespread adoption of these CCS techniques, combined with robust monitoring techniques and Government regulation."

There have been some critics of this technology, who say that the technology is very costly and implementing it could be waste of money, that its benefits are not established, that it is very risky to implement it etc[6] However the International Energy Agency (IEA) and Massachusetts Institute of Technology (MIT) have supported this technology. The Global Status of CCS: February, 2014[7] highlights as follows:

- As of February 2014 there are 21 large-scale projects in operation or construction - a 50% increase since 2011. These have the capacity to capture up to 40 million tonnes of CO_2 per annum, equivalent to 8 million cars being taken off the road.
- Six projects, with a combined capture capacity of 10 million tonnes of CO_2 per annum, are in advanced stages of development planning and may take a final investment decision during 2014.
- The world's first two power sector projects with CCS will begin operation in North America in 2014.
- The Middle East has the world's first large-scale CCS project in the iron and steel sector move into construction.
- China has doubled the number of CCS projects since 2011 with 12 large-scale CCS projects.

References:

1. UNEP (http://www.unep.org/climatechange/mitigation)

2. Focus Mitigation (http://unfccc.int/focus/mitigation/items/7169.php):

3. AR4 SYR Synthesis Report Summary for Policymakers (http://www.ipcc.ch/publications_and _dataar4/syr/en/spms4.html)

4. UNEP-Climate Change-Mitigation-Introduction (file:///D:/Documents and Settings/Admin/Desktop/-Climate..)

5. What is CCS? The Carbon Capture and Storage Association (CCSA) (http://www.ccsassociation.org/what –is ccs/)

6. Carbon Capture and Storage Pros and Cons (http://globalwarmingisrael.com/2009/07/16/carbon-capture-and -storage)

7. The Global Status of CCS: February 2014|Global Carbon Capture (http://www.globalccsinstitute.com/publications/global-status-ccs-fe..)

Chapter 18

CLIMATE CHANGE
AND FORESTS

*As each tree falls, so does the earth's ability to heal itself and
to adapt to the effects of our changing climate-*

Hilary Benn, Secretary of State for the Environment,
Food and Rural Affairs, UK. Addressing Copenhagen COP,
December, 2009.

Forests cover 31 percent of the world's land surface, just
over 4 billion hectares. According to FAO, deforestation
was at its highest rate in the 1990s, when each year the
world lost on average 16 million hectares of forests. At the
same time, forest expanded in some places, either through
planting or natural processes, bringing the global net loss
of forest to 8.3 million hectares per year. In the first decade
of this century, the rate of deforestation was slightly lower,
but still, a disturbingly high 13 million hectares were
destroyed annually. As forest expansion remained stable,
the global net forest loss between 2000 and 2010 was 5.2
million hectares per year[1].

"Forests are essential for life. Three hundred million
people worldwide live in forests and 1.6 billion depend

on them for their livelihoods. Forests provide habitat for a vast array of plants and animals, many which are still undiscovered. They protect our watersheds. They inspire wonder and provide places for recreation. They supply the oxygen we need to survive. They provide the timber for products we use every day. Forests are so much more than a collection of trees. Forests are home to 80% of the world's terrestrial biodiversity. These ecosystems are complex web of organisms that include plants, animals, birds, insects, fungi and bacteria. Forests take many forms depending upon their latitude, local soils, rainfall and prevailing temperatures[2].

Peatlands and mangroves: Peatland forests cover about 3 per cent of the Earth's land area but store as much as one-third of all soil carbon. Similarly, carbon density in mangrove forests is more than four times higher than in upland tropical forests[3].

According to the UNFCCC[4] forests present a significant global carbon stock. Global forest vegetation stores 283 Gt of carbon in its biomass, 38 Gt in dead wood and 317 Gt in soils(top 30 cm) and litter. The total carbon content of forest ecosystems has been estimated 638 Gt for 2005, which is more than the amount of carbon in the entire atmosphere. This standing carbon is combined with a gross terrestrial uptake of carbon, which was estimated at 2.4 Gt a year, a good deal of which is sequestered by forests. Further, based on IPCC report the UNFCCC Fact Sheet (22)[5] says that deforestation is the second largest source of carbon dioxide. "When forests are cleared for agriculture or development, most of the carbon burned or decomposing trees escapes to the atmosphere. There is a great deal of uncertainty about emissions from deforestation and other land-use changes, but it is estimated that 800 million to 2.4 billion tonnes of carbon are released globally every year".

WWF reports[6] more drastically:

- "Between 12-15 million hectares of forest are lost each year. Deforestation is responsible for up to 20% of all carbon emissions globally.
- Tropical forests, where deforestation is most prevalent, hold more than 210 Gt of carbon.
- Eighty seven per cent of global deforestation occurs in just 10 countries, with Brazil and Indonesia accounting for 51% of emission from forest loss.

Role of forests in climate change mitigation and adaptation. Forests are planted, protected and managed to derive many benefits from them like production of wood, protection of soil, water and other environmental services, habitat for wildlife, conservation of biodiversity, provision of socio-cultural services, livelihood support and poverty alleviation. No citation is needed to know benefits of trees in providing oxygen to the atmosphere. We have learnt in school days that trees act as air filters. Using carbon dioxide from the air, sunlight, and water, they create their own food (glucose, a sugar) in a process called **photosynthesis**. Byproducts of photosynthesis include oxygen and water. Imagine hundred trees, thousands trees or million trees doing this. Thus, for climate change mitigation forests have a crucial role of sequestration of carbon. On average, a planted forest in a temperate zone can sequester about 4 tonnes of carbon per hectare per year[7].

Forests, when sustainably managed, can have a central role in climate change mitigation and adaptation. By strengthening forest management practices countries can achieve sustainable forest management, which is an effective framework for forest-based climate change mitigation and adaptation. Sustainable forest management also contributes to food security, poverty alleviation, economical development, and sustainable land use, in the wider context of sustainable development. Good forest management secures the survival of forest ecosystems and enhances their environmental, socio-cultural and economic functions. It can both maximize forests' contribution to climate change mitigation and help forests and forest-dependent people adapt to new conditions caused by climate change. Improved forest management practices for climate change mitigation and adaptation should be planned and implemented in tandem, as they are closely linked[8].

According to FAO, forests have four major roles in climate change: they currently contribute about one-sixth of global carbon emissions, when cleared, overused or degraded; they react sensitively to a changing climate; when managed sustainably, they produce wood-fuels as a benign alternative to fossil fuels; and finally they have the potential **to absorb about one-tenth of global carbon emissions projected for the first half of this century into their biomass, soils and products and store them-in principle in perpetuity**[9].

Trees are planted for many purposes by the farmers alongside their farms, for horticulture, in the gardens, for beauty, shade and as social forestry alongside the roadside, in the compounds, lawns etc. These trees (outside forests) along with the benefits (fruit, fodder, timber) for which they are planted, can also have an important role in climate change mitigation and adaptation, through diversified land-use practices, livelihoods and sources of income, and through enhancement of agricultural productivity and buffering against weather-related production losses, enhancing resilience against climate impacts in farming systems

UNFCCC's efforts: Since the 13th Conference of Parties (COP 13) the UNFCCC in Bali in 2007, the UNFCCC has progressively recognized the package of measures now known as **REDD+**, which stands for Reducing Emissions from Deforestation and Forest Degradation, as well as the conservation and sustainable management of forests, and the enhancement of forest carbon stocks in developing countries' forests. At COP 16 in Durban, in 2011, negotiators agreed on monitoring guidelines as safeguards for REDD+ implementation and on the means for developing estimates of emissions that would have occurred in the absence of REDD+ (i.e. reference emission levels)[10].

Sources of Financing: Sources for financing have emerged to support forest-related mitigation efforts, including the Clean Development Mechanism (CDM) under the Kyoto Protocol and voluntary carbon markets, and, more recently, the REDD+ Partnership, the Forest Carbon Partnership Facility (FCPF) and the Forest Investment Programme (FIP) of the Strategic Climate Fund. REDD+ activities are also supported by bilateral and NGO funding.

Various funds managed by the Global Environment Facility (e.g. the Adaptation Fund) as well as other support – through multilateral, bilateral and NGO channels provide financial assistance for climate change adaptation of forests, forestry and forest-dependent people. The need for funding for adaptation measures is growing, as recognized in the Copenhagen Accord, which places equal weight on mitigation and adaptation.

NGOs in developing countries may contact FAO for support for forestry projects. For FAO's support contact: www.fao. org/forestry/tof

References:

1. Eco-Economy Indicators-Forest Cover| Earth Policy Institute (http://www.earth-policy.org/indicators/C56)

2. World Wildlife Fund- Forests (http://worldwildlife. org/habitats/forests)

3. Donato, D.et al.2011 Mangroves among the most carbon-rich forests in the tropics. Nature Geoscience 4, 293297 as cited in the Fact Sheet of the Centre for International Forestry Research (CIFOR), No. 5 November, 2012-Mitigation (www.cifor.org/fileadmin/ factsjeet/R10+20 Fact sheet-Mitigation pdf)

4. Importance of Forest Ecosystems-UNFCCC (www. unfccc/resource/docs/publications/forest_erg pdf).

5. UNFCCC Climate Change Fact Sheet 22 (http://unfccc. int/essential_background_publications_html)

6. WWF-Reducing emissions from deforestation and forest degradation (http://wwf.panda.org/ what_we_do/footprint/forest_climate2/forests)

7. FAO-Managing Forests for Climate Change (www.fao.
   org/docrep/013/11960 e/1960 e 00.pdf).

8. *Ibid*

9. FAO-Forestry and climate change (http://fao.org/
   forestry/climatechange53459/en)

10. *op.cit* Fact Sheet of CIFOR

Chapter 19

CLIMATE CHANGE AND GENDER EQUALITY

Climate Change emerged as an environmental issue and discussions about it were the exclusive domain of scientists and experts in atmospheric science. However as the assessment reports of the Intergovernmental Panel on Climate Change came one after the other, and the effects of climate change are felt all over the world, it was realized that its effects are many and grave and it is equally a socio-economic problem. The United Nations Framework Convention on Climate Change (UNFCCC), which was set up in 1994 to take joint efforts at the world level to tackle the threat of climate change, in its guidelines on how to prepare National Adaptation Plans for Action gave instructions on gender agenda. Similarly, as the awareness of climate change increased the gender approach for climate change gained ground in the Conference of Parties. There have been initiatives in the UN systems and otherwise, which highlighted the need to bring the policies and action plans on sustainable and climate change with a gender perspective A few such developments are as under: However it would fit in here if what the terms 'gender', 'gender equality' and 'gender approach' imply are specified here.

Gender refers to the differences in socially constructed roles and opportunities associated with being a man or a woman and the interactions and social relations between men and women. Gender determines what is expected, permitted and valued in a woman or a man in a determined context.

Gender equality refers to the equal rights, responsibilities and opportunities of women and men and girls and boys. Equality between men and women is seen both as a human rights issue and as a precondition for, and indicator of sustainable people centered development.

The gender approach provides the theoretical and methodological instrument to analyze gender relations, to understand their dynamics in specific contexts, such as climate change, and build proposals to promote equity.

The gender equity approach presupposes the recognition of the diversity of gender associated with age, ethnic group and socio-economic condition, among others.

What is the origin of gender inequality? Inequality has its origins in development models that were used to build present societies. Social assessment of individuals based on their gender has led to an unfair distribution of accessible resources and opportunities and, therefore, of the possibilities for participation in the benefits of development.

Reference: UNDP Gender Equality Strategy 2008-2011 as cited in the feature Climate change and gender equality (http://www.unesco.org/new/en/unesco/themes/gender-equality/themes/climate-change/).

Box 19

UN and its bodies and conventions on concern for women in the context of climate change:

1. Established on 21 June, 1946 the **Commission on the Status of Women** CSW) is a functional commission of the United Nations Economic and Social Council (ECOSOC). It is the principal global policy-making body dedicated exclusively to gender equality and advancement of women. Every year, representatives of Member States gather at United Nations Headquarters in New York to evaluate progress on gender equality, identify challenges, set global standards and formulate concrete policies to promote gender equality and women's empowerment worldwide. From 2002 the Commission has continued to promote awareness of the links between gender, disaster and climate change[1]

2. Established in 1991 the **Women's Environment & Development Organization(WEDO)** has to its credit many international conferences and initiatives, including the World Women's Congress for a Healthy Planet, bringing together more than 1500 women from 83 countries to work jointly on a strategy for the UN Conference on Environment and Development (UNCED) held in Rio de Janeiro, Brazil, in 1992. Agenda 21 at this conference paved the way for future action priorities to achieve sustainable development from then into the twenty-first century[2.]

3. The United Nations Development Programme, in its report of 2005, took stock of UNDP's efforts to develop and implement gender mainstreaming policies; and to assess the overall performance of

UNDP in gender mainstreaming and the promotion of gender equality in the last ten years. The evaluation is primarily forward-looking, responding to corporate concerns to increase the effectiveness of the organization's gender mainstreaming policies and strategies. This report and its Gender Equality Strategy 2008-11 inter alia, clearly defined the gender approach and the related terms[3].

4. Launched in partnerships with the UNDP and UNEP, and with support from the Governments of Finland and Denmark, **the Global Gender and Climate Alliance** (GGCA) was launched in 2007 at UNFCCC, COP 13 In Bali. It is a network of 13 UN Agencies and 25 civil society organizations, working together to ensure that climate change decision-making, policies and initiatives, at all levels, are gender responsive[4].

5. Prior to the Conference of Parties 13 (COP 13) of UNFCCC held in Bali, Indonesia, in 2007, representatives of the International Union for Conservation of Nature (IUCN), United Nations Development Programme (UNDP) and Womens' Environment and Development Organization (WEDO) came together to address this emerging issue of gender and climate change. The result was the formation of the Global Gender and Climate Alliance (GGCA)[5]-

6. In the framework of the UNFCCC COP 13, there were efforts to promote incorporation of the gender theme. In the meeting of 11 December, 2007 of Network of Women Ministers and Leaders for Environment called upon the Parties and the UNFCCC Secretariat to bring the agenda into the domain of decision making of the Conference of Parties.

The advocates for gender and climate change led several events during the COP 14 (2008) held at Poznan at the main event and side events, which raised awareness about the gendered impacts of climate change and resulted in greater delegate support to address the dire need to include a gender strategy in the UNFCCC.

COP 18 in Doha- December 2012

The efforts of those fighting for gender justice in action on climate change yielded fruits in the form of the Decision 23/CP.18 at this COP. An excerpt of the same is as below[6]: [Items 1,2,8,9,14 &15].

"Promoting gender balance and improving the participation of women in UNFCCC negotiations and in the representation of Parties in bodies established pursuant to the Convention or the Kyoto Protocol FCCC/CP/2012/8/Add.3 48

1. *Agrees* that additional efforts need to be made by all Parties to improve the participation of women in bodies established pursuant to the Convention and the Kyoto Protocol as envisaged in decision 36/CP.7;
2. *Decides* to enhance decision 36/CP.7 by adopting a goal of gender balance in bodies established pursuant to the Convention and the Kyoto Protocol, in order to improve women's participation and inform more effective climate change policy that addresses the needs of women and men equally;

8. *Requests* the secretariat to maintain information on the gender composition of constituted bodies established under the Convention and the Kyoto Protocol, including information on the representation of women from regional groups, to gather information on the gender composition of delegations to sessions under the Convention and the Kyoto Protocol and to report this information to the Conference of the Parties for its consideration on an annual basis, in order to enable the tracking of progress made towards the goal of gender balance in advancing gender-sensitive climate policy;

9. *Decides* to add the issue of gender and climate change as a standing item on the agenda of sessions of the Conference of the Parties to allow the Conference of the Parties to consider the information referred to in paragraph 8 above;

10. *Requests* the secretariat to organize, in conjunction with the nineteenth session of the Conference of the Parties, an in-session workshop on gender balance in the UNFCCC process, gender-sensitive climate policy and capacity-building activities to promote the greater participation of women in the UNFCCC process;

11. *Further requests* the secretariat to compile those submissions into a miscellaneous document for consideration by the Conference of the Parties at its nineteenth session;

12. *Requests that* the actions of the secretariat called for in this decision be undertaken subject to the availability of financial resources.

13. *Invites* the Conference of the Parties serving as the meeting of the Parties to the Kyoto Protocol to endorse this decision."

References:

1. Commission on the Status of Women. (http://www.un.org/womenwatch/daw/csw/57sess.htm)

2. Gender at the Earth Summit, Box 10,Gender equality in the context of climate change (www.un.org/womenwatch/downloads/Resource Guide English-FINAL PDF)

3. Evaluation of Gender Mainstreaming in UNDP (web.undp.org/evaluation/documents/eogendermainstreaming/pdf)

4. Global Gender and Climate Alliance (http://www.wedo.org/category/themes/sustainable -)

5. *ibid*

6. Conference of Parties 18 (para 2 and 11 of decision 23/CP.18 (https://unfccc.int/gender and climate change/items/7516.php#infocus)

Chapter 20

CLIMATE CHANGE FUNDS FOR ADAPTATION AND MITIGATION

The United Nations Framework Convention on Climate Change (UNFCCC) is a comprehensive convention (treaty) of the nations to collectively act upon the challenge of climate change. Kyoto Protocol is its *update*. Article 11 of the Convention is in regard to financial support to the developing countries and other least developed countries. In brief, the article concerns itself with-

- Provision of financial resources on a grant or concessional basis.
- Accountable to the Conference of Parties (its supreme body)
- Equitable and balanced representation of all Parties within a transparent system of governance.
- Agreement of the Conference of Parties (COP) and the entity or entities entrusted with the operation of the financial mechanism on the arrangements.

A key element of the Convention that enjoins its members to protect the climate system is- "**on the basis of equality and in accordance with their common but differentiated**

responsibilities and respective capacities." The convention, therefore, states that developed countries should provide 'new and additional' funds to help developing countries meet their treaty commitments. The Convention's 'financial mechanism' is a major source of funding. Its role is to transfer funds and technology to developing countries on a grant or concessional basis.

The Convention initially assigned this role to the Global Environment Facility (GEF). In 1999 the COP decided to entrust the GEF with this responsibility on an ongoing basis and to review the financial mechanism every four years. In 2001 the COP agreed to the need to establish two new funds under the Convention- a **Special Climate Change Fund (SCCF)** and a **fund for the least developed countries-** to help developing countries adapt to climate change impacts, obtain clean technologies, and limit the growth in their emissions. These funds are to be managed within the GEF framework. The COP also agreed to establish an Adaptation Fund under the 1997 Kyoto Protocol[1].

The Global Environment Facility (GEF) was set up earlier than the Convention came into being. It was the Brundtland Commission (1987) that had first discussed the need for a mechanism to support projects benefitting the environment. The GEF was subsequently launched with the World Bank, the United Nations Development Programme (UNDP), and the United Nations Environment Programme (UNEP), as implementing agencies. GEF brings together 173 member governments, leading development institutions, the scientific community, and a wide spectrum of private sector and NGOs on behalf of a common global environment agenda. GEF funds complement regular development assistance, offering developing countries the opportunity to incorporate environmentally-friendly features that address global environmental concerns. For example, if a country invests in a new power plant to promote economic development, the GEF may provide additional, or incremental funds needed to buy equipment for reducing the emissions of greenhouse. The projects must be country-driven and based on national priorities that support sustainable development. The focal areas covered by GEF include, climate change, biological diversity, international waters, protection of ozone layer, combating land degradation and fighting organic pollutants. focal areas. Funding proposals to the GEF are to be submitted through one of the three implementing agencies, viz. UNDP, UNEP and the World Bank. The GEF Secretariat oversees the work programme and helps to ensure that projects comply with COP decisions and with GEF programming strategies and policies. Once approved, projects are carried out by a wide range of agencies, such as government ministries, non-governmental organizations, UN bodies, regional multilateral institutions, and private firms. The final authority for all funding decisions and operational, programmatic, and strategic issues is vested in the GEF Council. The Council consists of 32 of GEF's 166 members and meets semi-annually, while the Assembly of all participating countries meets every three years[2 and 3].

Adaptation Finance

Adaptation Fund

The Adaptation Fund was established in 2001 to finance concrete adaptation projects and programmes in developing country Parties to the Kyoto Protocol that are particularly vulnerable to the adverse effects of climate change. The Fund is financed from the share of proceeds on the <u>Clean Development Mechanism (CDM)</u> project activities and other sources of funding. The share of proceeds amounts to 2% of <u>certified emission reductions (CERs)</u> issued for a CDM project activity. The Adaptation Fund is supervised and managed by the **Adaptation Fund Board** (AFB). The AFB is composed of 16 members and 16 alternates and meets at least twice a year.

Activities supported include[4]:

- Water resources management, land management, agriculture, health, infrastructure development, fragile ecosystems;
- Improving the monitoring of diseases and vectors affected by climate change, and related forecasting and early-warning systems, and in this context improving disease control and prevention;
- Supporting capacity building, including institutional capacity, for preventive measures, planning, preparedness and management of disasters relating to climate change;
- Strengthening existing and, where needed, establishing national and regional centres and information networks for rapid response to extreme weather events, utilizing information technology as much as possible.

Special Climate Change Fund (SCCF)[5]

The Special Climate Change Fund (SCCF) was created in 2001 to address the specific needs of developing countries under the UNFCCC. It covers the incremental costs of interventions to address climate change relative to a development baseline. Adaptation to climate change is the top priority of the SCCF, although it can also support technology transfer and its associated capacity building activities. The SCCF is intended to catalyze and leverage additional finance from bilateral and multilateral sources, and is administered by the Global Environment Facility.

The SCCF has two focus areas (1) Adaptation and (2) Transfer of technologies Its governing instrument also allows it to support (3) projects on energy, transport, industry, agriculture, forestry, and waste management; and (4) activities to assist developing countries whose economies are highly dependent on income generated from the production, processing, and export or on consumption of fossil fuels and associated energy-intensive products in diversifying their economies.

Least Developed Countries Fund[6]

The Least Developed Countries Fund (LDCF) was established to meet the adaptation needs of least developed countries (LDCs). Specifically the LDCF has financed the preparation and implementation of National Adaptation Programs of Action (NAPAs) to identify priority adaptation actions for a country based on existing information. The Least Developed Countries Fund is administered by the Global Environment Facility.

The LDCF aims to address the needs of the 48 LDCs which are particularly vulnerable to the adverse impacts of climate change. As a priority, the LDCF supports the preparation and the implementation of the National Adaptation Programs of Action (NAPAs), which are country-driven strategies that identify the immediate needs of LDCs in order to adapt to climate change.

The LDCF supports the preparation of NAPAs which supports LDCs to identify priority activities that respond to their urgent and immediate needs to adapt to climate change. It can also fund NAPA implementation, including the design, development, and implementation of projects on the ground.

Mitigation Finance

The text of the UNFCCC Article reads:

"The ultimate objective of this Convention and any related legal instruments that the Conference of the Parties may adopt is to achieve, in accordance with the relevant provisions of the Convention, stabilization of greenhouse gas concentrations in the atmosphere at a level that would prevent dangerous anthropogenic interference with the climate system....."

Mitigation involves a process of curbing greenhouse gas emissions from human activities. The theme of mitigation permeates the Kyoto Protocol. On the guiding principles of the Convention, the developed countries are enjoined to provide technology and funds to the developing countries in their efforts to curb the emissions of greenhouse gases. International climate finance can assist developing countries to implement mitigation actions including renewable energy and energy efficiency programmes, and more sustainable transport systems.

There are five funds for mitigation[7] launched in the year shown in bracket.

1) Clean Technology Fund (CTF) (2008).
2) Global Environmental Facility Trust(GEF 4) (2006)
3) Global Environmental Facility Trust (GEF 5) (2010)
4) Global Energy Efficiency Renewable Energy Fund (GEEREF) (2008)
5) Scaling-Up Renewable Energy Program for Low Income Countries (SREP) (2009)

References:

1. UNFCCC Climate Change Information Sheet 18 (https://unfccc.int/essential_background_publications_ht).

2. *Ibid*

3. Ministry of Environment & Forests, Govt.. of India (http://www.moef.nic.in/divisions/ic/gef/gef.htm).

4. Adaptation Fund UNFCCC (http://unfccc.int/cooperation_and_support/financial_mechnism/adap..)

5. Special Climate Change Fund (http://unfccc.int/cooperation_and_support/financial_mechnism/spec..)

6. LDC Fund (http://unfccc.int/cooperation_and_support/financial_mechanism/leas..).

7. UNFCCC-Climate finance portal (http://unfccc.int/focus/climate_finance/items/7001.php)

Chapter 21

WHAT CAN INDIVIDUALS AND HOUSEHOLDS DO TO TACKLE CLIMATE CHANGE?

*We have a responsibility to look after
our planet. It is our only home.*

-Dalai Lama

Now that the IPCC has confirmed that there is human hand in the climate change, therefore, it will be through human hand that it can be tackled, managed, mitigated and adapted to. The world has assigned the task of taking action on the UNFCCC. The UNFCCC calls all the countries to come together in the Conference of Parties held every year to deliberate upon and decide course of action on mitigation and adaptation. The countries, in turn, draw policies and announce measures in this respect. Theoretically this looks fine. Side by side, there is another truth that unless people (most of them-every one of them) feel concerned and act upon no policy can succeed. Small things, mundane matters, day to day activities if done by all with a little needed care, can make a **big** difference. There are such innumerable measures that can make the task of tackling climate change easy. These are avoiding waste; bringing about economy and efficiency in the use of power, energy, fuel, paper, water etc. and this has a direct relevance to climate change. There is a huge literature available on these things so that if many of them are to be mentioned and explained then it will make a book, more in size than this book. As such, the author had to exercise utmost economy in mentioning such measures in broad terms only.

Family Power: The whole humanity is divided into billions of families. A family cooks food, uses electricity, consumes power, uses fuel. How to inform them on doing these things wisely? For this purpose in India an organization called **Petroleum Conservation Research Association (PCRA)** has been set up. This organization, through a range of its activities, campaigns creates awareness of using domestic fuel and other things wisely. The author feels that many developing countries and all the least developed countries, if they are not having such an organization, should set up such an organization. They may use the information put up on its website (http://www.pcra.org). A few of the tips given by the PCRA are as under.

Cooking. *Remember*: A few minutes of planning ensures a big fuel saving- Light your stove after you have kept all the ingredients within your reach and ready for cooking, Pressure cooking saves fuel and time. Use separators in the pressure cooker to cook different items at the same time. Use optimum quantity of water. Surplus water consumes additional fuel which could otherwise be saved. Reduce the flame once boiling starts. Soak before cooking. Sizeable savings in fuel are possible if you soak cereals in water before cooking. Shallow wide vessels save fuel. Hide the flame with broad bottomed vessels. Do not use vessels which are narrow as they allow the flame to creep up on the sides. Always place a lid on an open cooking vessel or pan. This saves heat loss. Use the small burner or lower flame more often. A bright, steady flame means efficient burning. If you see an orange, yellow or non-uniform flame, clean the burner or wick as the case may be. All frozen food be allowed to reach room temperature before cooking. Imagine if 10 million families in a country are made aware of these small things and if they save just 15 units in a month, the total saving would amount to 15x 1000000=15000000 units[1].

Good Driving Habits. Tests on Indian cars prove that you can get up to 40% extra mileage at this speed. Avoid accelerating or decelerating unnecessary. Keep your engine healthy. Tests have shown that you can save about 6% by servicing your vehicle regularly. Use of bi-metallic spark plugs saves over 1.5% fuel and reduces exhaust emissions too. Get your car serviced at every 5000 kms Follow manufacturer's recommendation. Use chokes briefly only when necessary. In cold regions, install engine-heating system. Stopping frequently wastes fuel. When you slam on the brakes, a lot of useful energy is wasted in the form of heat. A good driver anticipates stops. Check wheel alignment at regular intervals. Keep your foot off the clutch. Riding the clutch causes loss of energy and damages clutch-linings. Clean air filter regularly. Dust causes rapid wear of engine components and increases fuel consumption. Under inflated tyres increase rolling resistance, this leads to higher petrol consumption. When stopping car, engine should also be stopped. Use recommended grade of oil[2]

Energy Conservation Measures: Energy conservation measures are not a new thing. They are devised in almost all countries and organizations. But the fact remains that they are not fully implemented. So, need is to reinforce from time to time and creating vigilance in following them. Lighting consumes about 40% of the energy used in office buildings. Fortunately, there are excellent technologies that have been developed to reduce the amount of energy needed to light office building[3]. It is a matter of common knowledge that compact fluorescent lamp (CFL) is much more energy saver than the incandescent light bulb[4]. LED lighting is the latest one in power saving.

Office Equipments: Office equipments use a substantial amount of energy. It is always better to buy energy starred equipments. A habit should be cultivated among users to switch off the equipment when not in actual use. Install timers and occupancy sensors that will turn office equipment, lighting and HVAC systems off automatically when they are not needed. Make sure that equipments are turned off on leaving office at nights and weekends. This is more particularly needed for copy machines and printers, as even in their sleep mode they burn 30 to 40 watts of electricity. Low cost plug-in 7-day timers are available that automatically shut off printers at night and weekends[5]

Computers. Laptops computers use 90% less energy than regular computers. So while replacing older machineries, they are the best option. Similarly, **LED Screens** of the computer monitors use 90% less energy and occupy less space. They have become popular and their prices have come down. Unless specifically needed large monitors be avoided. A 17" monitor uses 35% more power than a 14" monitor[6].

Economic Use of Paper: Papers are enormously used in administration, management, communication, documentation, judiciary, education and most of the activities of modern life. This is an age of paper. **Going**

Demat. Demat, a short form of *dematerializing* i.e. transforming material (solid) form into virtual form. This is a form of transacting, keeping a record of transaction and its documentation in electronic form only. In most of the countries, 99% of virgin paper comes from trees.

- Make two-sided copies, whenever possible. This should be made a rule, and one-sided copy an exception. Blank sides of spare papers should be used for scribbling pads, note-taking and printing of drafts.

- In organizations substantial day to day communication, exchange of date, information etc. can be conveniently done through email, which makes for quick transfer. It also gets saved on email, without the use of paper.

- Send electronic greeting cards to your clients, prospects and colleagues instead of paper cards. A salutary development is that use of SMS through mobiles has caught up.

- Governments should give impetus to recycling of paper and take measures to sustain recycling market. Paper industry has developed tree-free paper kind, which needs to be used appropriate purposes.

- A habit should be cultivated not to print every memo or email one receives. Such emails as are required for future reference should be saved.

- Reusing packaging material saves more resources and energy than recycling.

Avoiding waste of water: Great amount of energy is used in bringing water from the reservoirs to the cities. It becomes incumbent to use this precious thing wisely.

The fact is that water is one of the highly wasted things. Almost in all the city water supply there are leakages and other wastes. At the household level there are many wastes of water. Precious potable drinking water is used for washing, gardening and flushing. There are many areas for improvement in water harvesting, distribution and use. Rainwater harvesting is a strongly suggested measure in cities. There is great need of water re-use and recycling of kitchen and bathroom used water for treatment and use for non-potable purposes like car washing, gardening etc. These are most relevant for water stressed countries.

Summing Up:

> Most of above measures are well known, but not properly implemented. If earnestly implemented by these small things can make a big difference to the collective efforts of combating climate change. This can be done when the concern of the detrimental effects would permeate as mass awareness.

One of the chief objectives of this book is to disseminate awareness of avoiding wastages, which look a small thing but if adopted by the billions of people can make a big difference.

References:

1. Welcome to PCRA (http://www.pcra.org/English/domestic/lastLong.htm)

2. Welcome to PCRA (http://www/pcra.org/English/transport/drivingHabits.htm

3. Energy Saving Measures for Building Tenants (www.accenv.com/documents/Energy Measures for Tenants.pdf)

4. Wikipedia.

5. Energy Saving Measures for Tenants, *op.cit*

6. Note pad given to officers of the DSB Bank, Mumbai.

Chapter 22

INDIA AND CLIMATE CHANGE

[Under Green India Mission, India has embarked upon greening the country. India. Photo 22. Pic. Mr. Sanjay Bale).

According to Census of India (2011), 833 million, i.e. 68.84 per cent of Indian population lives in rural areas. Indian peninsula has a large coastline of 7517 kms. About 800 million population of India is engaged in agriculture and allied activities – farming, cultivation, plantation, horticulture, animal husbandry, poultry, fisheries, forestry etc. which are climate sensitive sectors. According to the Ministry of Earth Sciences, Government of India. *"Climate change will, in all likelihood, predispose India to enhanced threats from natural hazards linked to the atmosphere and oceans, besides stressing the availability of water and health of our key natural managed ecosystems"*[1]. Compared to the

0.74° C increase in the global average surface temperature between 1906-2005 (IPCC), an analysis of data done by the India Meteorological Department for the period 1901-2009 suggests that annual mean temperature for India, as a whole, has **risen by 0.56°C during the said period**.[2]

From the 13th COP held at Bali, between 3-15 December, 2007 the main focus was on long term cooperation post -2012 when the first commitment period of the Kyoto Protocol was to expire. (It now stands extended up to 2020). In 2008 in the COP 14, held at Poznan, Poland it was concluded that a commitment in the shape of an effective international response to climate change will be agreed at COP 15 in Copenhagen in December 2009.

In view of these developments India had to take an official stand in the Conference of Parties (15) in Copenhagen held during 7-18 December, 2009. The Public Diplomacy Division of the Ministry of External Affairs, Government of India came up with a booklet **"THE ROAD TO COPANHAGEN: India's Position on Climate Change Issues[4]"** A few excerpts from the booklet are as below to make the India's stand clear:

"We expect that Copenhagen will result in an ambitious outcome, representing a cooperative global response to the challenge of climate change, but an outcome which is also fair and equitable. It must be in accordance with the principle of **common but differentiated responsibilities and respective capabilities**, a principle that the entire international community has, by consensus, enshrined in the UNFCCC, concluded in 1992 at the historic Rio Summit."

Similarly, a few excerpts from the speech by Mr. Jairam Ramesh, Minister for Environment and Forest, delivered at COP 16, at Cancun, on December 8, 2010 are briefly reproduced here. Update on Copenhagen statements-

"Firstly, we have announced that we will reduce emissions intensity of India's GDP by 20-25% by the year 2020 on a 2005 reference level.

"Secondly, we have taken firm steps to diversify our energy fuel mix. (Substantial increase in solar power capacity, doubling of nuclear power, expansion of natural gas in power production).

"Thirdly, we are pursuing aggressive strategies on forestry and coastal management (E.g. Launching of an ambitious Green India Mission to increase the quality and quantity of forest cover in 10 million hectares of land and a major new programme on coastal zone management).

"Fourthly, we have set up an elaborate Indian Network for Comprehensive Climate Change Assessment, an Indian IPCC as it were.

"Fifthly, we are actively engaging in partnership with our neighbors and other countries to deal with climate change.

GHG Emission Measurement

India's first GHG emissions inventory was made in 2004 as a part of its National Communication. India has now proactively estimated its GHG inventory for the year 2007 in view of the need for GHG emission assessment to be made on a scientific and regular basis. The assessment for 2007 was carried out under the aegis of the Indian Network for Climate Change Assessment (INCCA). The GHG inventory has been prepared by scientists and experts drawn from a network of a diverse mix of institutions across the country having the capacity to generate information on the GHG emission inventories by sources and removals by sinks from Energy, Industry, Agriculture, Land use, Land-use Change and Forestry and Waste sectors on a regular basis. These institutions comprise national research institutions, technical institutions, universities, industry associations, non-Governmental Organizations and the private sector. Other than estimating the GHG inventories, these institutions also collected activity data from relevant sources, and are also involved in the process of generating country specific emission factors. Developing country specific emission factors has been the thrust since the First National Communication process began, especially for the key emitting sources, as it makes the inventory more representative of the circumstances under which the emissions take place and the estimates more scientifically robust[5].

GHG emissions in 2007

India's GHG emissions are heavily influenced by the structure of its large and expanding economy, the limitations on its energy resources, as also its current status in terms of energy access. In 2007, India's greenhouse gas (GHG) emission by sources and removal by sinks were 1727.71 million tons of CO_2 equivalents (or 1904.73 million tones of CO_2 equivalents without land use, land use change and forestry), with the largest shares from electricity generation (38%), agriculture (18%) and other energy industries (12%)[6].

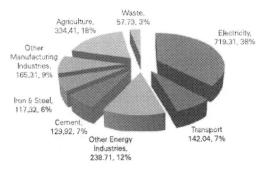

Fig. 22.1 Sectorwise greenhouse emissions in India.

Reference: Climate Change and 12th Five Year Plan, Planning Commission, Govt. of India.

Sources of greenhouse gas emissions from Indian agriculture

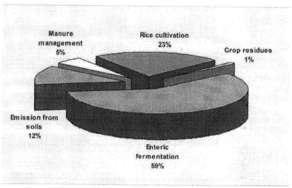

Figure 1. Sources of greenhouse gas emissions from Indian agriculture

Fig. 22.2 Reference: Climate Change and 12th Five Year Plan, Planning Commission, Govt. of India. (The document is in public domain)

- The emissions from Indian agriculture are likely to increase significantly in future due to our need to increase food production. The latter would require greater emphasis on application of fertilizers and other inputs. This, in a globally warm environment leads to increased emissions of nitrous oxides and other GHGs. Increased temperatures would lead to higher emissions even at the current level of fertilizer consumption. Despite this, the relative proportion of emissions from agriculture in India is likely to show considerable reduction in future because of larger emission growth in other sectors compared to agriculture[7].

Trends of GHG emission in India

GHG sources and sinks (4)	1990 (tCO$_2$e)	1994 (tCO$_2$e)	2000 (tCO$_2$e)	CAGR, % (1999-2000)
Total emissions	987,885	1,228,539	1,484,622	4.2
Industrial Processes	24,510	102,710	168,378	21.3
Per capita emissions	1.2	1.3	1.5	

CAGR = Compounded Annual Growth Rate

Inventorization of national GHG emissions related to various sectors like energy, industrial processes and product use, agriculture, forestry etc. would help analyze and implement opportunities for reducing the intensity of emissions, including energy management and product use efficiency initiatives. The Industrial Processes and Product Use (IPPU) sector includes GHG emissions produced as a direct by-product of non-energy industrial activities and the emissions involved during the non-energy use of materials which are produced by a process and used as a product in other processes. (In the Second National Communication (2012), Product Use sector is taken along with Industrial Processes sector)[8]

National Action Plan on Climate Change:[9]

On 30th June, 2008 Prime Minister Manmohan Singh released India's first **National Action Plan on Climate Change** outlining existing and future policies and programmes addressing climate change adaptation and mitigation. The Plan identifies core national missions-

1. National Solar Mission.
2. National Mission for Enhanced Energy Efficiency.
3. National Water Mission.
4. National Mission for Sustaining the Himalayan Eco-system.
5. Mission for Green India.
6. National Mission of Sustainable Agriculture
7. National Mission on Strategic Knowledge on Climate Change, India's stance stands justified

In the run-up to the 2015 deadline, the debate on emissions is now centered on these four major emitters. As per the World Carbon Report for 2013, China is the highest emitter (27.6%), followed by the USA (14.5%), European Union (9.6%) and India (6.7%). However, when it comes to per capita emission, the position is as follows.

Country	Share in world emission (2013)	Per capita emission (2013) Metric tonnes per person
China	27.6 %	7.2
USA	14.5 %	16
European Union	9.6 %	6.8
India	6.7 %	1.8

Recalling Article 2 of the UNFCCC, the one of the two chief objectives of UNFCCC to spare the developing countries from binding cuts in emissions was that the developing countries are fighting against poverty, hunger, diseases, lack of electricity to millions, as such any binding cut on emissions would adversely affect their struggles for improving quality of life of its citizens. There are many supporters for India's stand. To quote Dr. Robbie Andrew of the Centre for International Climate and Environment Research, Norway, "They (India) have so many things to focus on in that country, to ask them to pull back on emissions is a big problem." In the UN summit on climate change held in September, 2014 this year leaders acknowledged that climate action *should be undertaken within the context of efforts to eradicate extreme poverty and promote sustainable development.*

We need to change our lifestyles. Energy not consumed is the cleanest energy. Indian Prime Minister, Mr. Narendra Modi, while addressing the UN Summit on Climate Change on 27 September, 2014.

Box 22.3

The new government under the premiership of Mr. Narendra Modi has changed the name of the Ministry of Environment and Forests as the Ministry of Environment, Forests and Climate Change and has embarked upon ambitious emission cutting policies.

References:

1. Ministry of Earth Sciences, (www.tropmet.res.in/ Centre_for _Climate Change-Research.pdf.

2. Indian Meteorological Department. Climate Profile of India. Contribution to the Indian Network of Climate Change Assessment (NATIONAL COMMUNICATION-II) S D Attri and Ajit Tyagi,2010.

3. THE ROAD TO COPENHAGEN; India's Position on Climate Change Issues.

-the document prepared by the Public Diplomacy Division, Ministry of External Affairs, Government of India. (http://www.meanindia.nic.in)

4. Climate Change & 12th Five Year Plan. Report of the Sub-Group on Climate Change, Government of India, Planning Commission,(October 2011)

5. *Ibid*

6. *Ibid*

7. *Ibid*

9. *ibid*